New England's
NAUGHTY NAVY

This book is dedicated to Dick Lamby and Mike Cahill, shown below, the last two privateersmen of Salem, Massachusetts — they, however, plunder beneath the waves, unlike the privateersmen of old who plundered above them. They hold the first flag of the United States Navy, flown during the Revolutionary War by Rhode Island's Commodore Esek Hopkins, first Commander of the Continental fleet. The rattlesnake, conceived by Ben Franklin in 1754, represented the Thirteen Colonies, its head being New England. In 1775, Franklin revived the rattlesnake symbol, stating that, "the rattlesnake never begins an attack, nor once engaged, ever surrenders... She never wounds until she has generously given notice, even to her enemy... One of her rattles is incapable of producing sound; but ringing of thirteen together is sufficient to alarm the boldest... The rattlesnake is found in no other quarter of the globe than America."

Cover Photo: ISBN 0-916787-10-9

Painting of the U.S. Frigate **CONSTITUTION**, launched at Boston on October 21, 1797. Carrying 54 guns, she sailed and battled victoriously through 84 years of active service, and is now docked at the Navy Yard in Charlestown, Massachusetts - photo courtesy of the John Hancock Mutual Life Insurance Company, Boston, MA.

INTRODUCTION

"Massachusetts ships traffic with the West Indies, so that little is left for merchants residing in England to import into any of these Colonies," wrote Englishman Edward Randolph in 1676. *"Massachusetts even sends ships to Egypt, to the slave markets of West Africa, and yes,"* he added with disgust, *"even to the pirate headquarters of Madagascar."* Randolph was right, but an even greater offender in this *"trafficing"* was Rhode Island. In the late 1600s, over 120 Rhode Island vessels were active in the slave trade, each carrying about 100 slaves per voyage from Africa to the West Indies, where they were traded for molasses, which was shipped back to Newport to make rum, which in turn was sold to procure more slaves. At the same time, England boasted of having some 500 vessels occupied in slave trading, capable of carrying some 300 blacks apiece. Rhode Island, like Massachusetts, was also a pirate haven. In 1702, the Governor of Rhode Island reported that, *"all able-bodied men at Newport are away privateering,"* which in those days was referred to as *"left-handed pirating."* One of the world's most notorious pirates, Thomas Tew, started out as a Rhode Island privateersman, and famous pirate Captain William Kidd chose Rhode Island as one of his final ports-of-call, as did the treacherous Blackbeard. This was part of the *"trafficing with the West Indies,"* that English merchants continuously complained about.

About the same time that Randolph petitioned Parliament and the King to restrict New England merchants, Sir Josiah Child published a *"Discourse On Trade"* in London, which further emphasized Mother England's jealousy of her successful upstart offspring. *"New England is the most prejudicial plantation,"* he wrote. *"Of all American plantations, His Majesty has none so apt for the building of shipping as New England, nor any comparably so qualified of the breeding of seamen, not only by reason of the natural industry of that people, but principally by reason of their cod and mackerel fisheries; and in my poor opinion, there is nothing more prejudicial, and in prospect, more dangerous to any mother kingdom, than the increase of shipping in her colonies, plantations, and provinces..."* How right Sir Child was, but it was His Majesty and the British Parliament that increased this danger by inflicting a series of *"Navigation Acts"* on American merchants and seamen, assuring England's monopoly on sea trade. According to these *"Acts,"* desired American merchandise and foodstuffs had to be shipped to and sold in England and not in any other foreign port. Only lumber, salt, grain, and rum could be sold elsewhere by American merchants, but within specified strict limitations. Cargos of sugar, tobacco, indigo and cotton, delivered from one American colony to another, were heavily taxed by the English — all this brought great indignation in New England, turning honest merchants into smugglers.

New Englanders continued trading with whomever they pleased, and the West Indies became dependent on their trade. American merchants armed their vessels to defend against British battle-cruisers that were sent out from England to enforce the Navigation Acts. Throughout the early 1700s, when war raged in Europe and Canada, Americans were most successful in smuggling ventures and in illegal trade, oft-times with England's enemies. When peace came in 1764, the English enforced the Navigation Acts with renewed vengeance. Many New England merchant vessels were confiscated on the high seas, their captains and seamen imprisoned, or forced to sail on extended voyages without pay on English naval vessels — their captured cargos sold at auction in English ports. The Navigation Acts were constantly being revised, adding new revenues and restrictions on American imports and exports. The English had incurred a heavy debt during the war years, and Parliament believed the Americans, especially New Englanders, should pay for the long years of English military protection during the French and Indian War.

In the British Parliament, Charles Townshend, after successfully passing a new bill imposing further taxes on the sea-merchants of America, justified this action by saying, *"And now will these Americans, planted by our care, nourished up by our indulgence, until they are grown to a degree of strength and importance, and protected by our arms, will they grudge to contribute their mite to relieve us from the heavy burden we lie under?"* Another British parliamentarian, Colonel Issac Barre, stood up in opposition to Townshend and shouted, *"They, planted by your care? No! . . . . Your oppression planted them in America. They, nourished by your indulgence? No! . . . . They grew by your neglect to them. They, protected by your arms? No! . . . . They have nobly taken up arms in your defence, have exerted their valor amidst their constant and laborious industry. . . and believe me, that same spirit of freedom, which activated these people, will accompany them still."* Like Edward Randolph and Sir Josiah Child before him, Colonel Barre was right, but Townshend and his cronies merely chuckled at the thought that New England *"country bumpkins"* would *"activate"* in a *"spirit of freedom,"* — A few merchant seamen in little cargo ships, take on the British Navy, the greatest navy in the world, over a little tax on stamps and tea? You've got to be kidding?

I
THE TAKING OF LIBERTIES

The greatest aggravation to New Englanders and, especially, merchant mariners was when 29 British ships-of-the-line and war-sloops, some carrying 70-cannons, anchored in the harbors of America's most active shipping ports in 1768. Their mission was to capture and punish seamen and ship owners who attempted to smuggle merchandise and foodstuffs in and out of American ports without paying taxes to Mother England. Within a few months of their arrival, another problem arose, which further tormented the citizens of the port towns. Hundreds of British tars and marines, sick of the hard life aboard these men-of-war, deserted the military life the moment they got shore leave, most of them joining the crews of local merchantmen, where smuggling ventures brought them three times the pay they received as British sailors. To make up for their ever depleting crews, British officers allowed press-gangs to go ashore at night, entering taverns, pubs, and inns to capture New England sailors and fishermen, forcing them to join the British Navy as seamen. The Royal Navy had always been noted for pressing needed sailors from American ships, but now they were literally coming into New England homes to prey on their helpless subjects.

This pressing issue climaxed and almost sparked the eventual Revolution in early 1769, when Lieutenant Henry Panton, commander of the 20-gun **H.M.S. ROSE**, stationed off Marblehead, Massachusetts, attempted to press four Marblehead sailors into joining his crew. Panton, threatening to fire on the brigantine **PITT PACKET** as she returned to Marblehead Harbor from Europe, brought her along side the **ROSE** and his press-gang boarded her. The Yankees, wielding knives and harpoons, avoided capture by retreating to the forepeak of the **PITT PACKET**. As Lieutenant Panton, leading his crew, advanced on them, seaman Michael Corbet lashed out with a harpoon, shouting, *"You have no right to impress me."* The British rushed him and he released his harpoon, right through Panton's neck, killing him instantly. Corbet was shot in the arm. He and his mates were captured, put in irons and brought to Boston to face a special British Admiralty Court. A guilty verdict of *"piracy and murder on the high seas,"* with which all four mariners were charged, meant a date with the hangman. In the streets outside the court house, where less than a year later five New Englanders would be killed in cold blood by British Redcoats in the Boston Massacre, a large and boisterous crowd gathered. The most prominent New England attorney, James Otis, was to defend the

Marbleheaders before Chief Justice Thomas Hutchinson, but Otis never showed up. Earlier he had been clouted on the head with a cutlass by a British customs official, and was never right in the head again. His assistant, John Adams, took his place as defense attorney. Adams was ready to give a stirring speech, of which he later said, *"would have accelerated the Revolution,"* but Chief Justice Hutchinson never gave him a chance to speak. Hutchinson, who was then acting Governor and would become the Royal Governor of Massachusetts in 1771, realized impressment was illegal in America, according to British law. He also realized the little colony was about to revolt over the issue. His own home had been destroyed during the Stamp Act riot, some four years before. He knew that, unless his verdict on Corbet and his mates was just and wise, the mob would rise again, even with British marines anchored in the harbor. *"The killing of Lieutenant Panton was justifiable homicide,"* he announced to a surprised John Adams and his clients, *"It was in necessary defence."* On hearing the news, the crowd outside went wild with joy, hoisted the Marbleheaders to their shoulders, and all were off to the nearest tavern. The British Navy continued to impress sailors, but Hutchinson's wise decision had tempered the growing anger and hatred of the British, at least for awhile.

About the time of the **ROSE** incident off Marblehead, a group of sailors and dock workers of neighboring Salem decided to take the law into their own hands. Two British sympathizers, Tom Rowe and Bob Wood, had squealed to the British customs official at Salem that certain local sea captains had not paid lawful duty to His Majesty for goods smuggled into the harbor. About thirty of the seamen and dock workers captured Rowe and Wood and dragged them, screaming, to Salem Common. There, they plastered them with hot tar, then began beating them with a live goose, held by the neck, until goose feathers stuck to their chests, backs, and blackened faces. Then they placed the whimpering men in a cart, each with a sign attached to his chest, reading *"Informer"* and wheeled them out of town, threatening *"worse punishment"* if they ever returned to Salem.

At Hancock Wharf in Boston, some 15 miles from Salem, the sloop **LIBERTY**, with a cargo of wine from Madeira, silently slipped into dockside in the dead of the night. The Boston customs official, Thomas Kirk, was told by an informer that the **LIBERTY** had snuck into port, so he went to the wharf and boarded the sloop, *"to check the cargo and see to it that all duties were paid to His Majesty."* Four men slipped out of the shadows, grabbed Kirk from behind, and locked him below in a small cabin. *"I heard cargo being taken off the sloop,"* Kirk testified later, *"and no duties were paid."* When Kirk was released, after 100 pipes of smuggled wine were safely hidden in a warehouse, he went directly to Benjamin Hallowell, the Boston comptroller of customs. Hallowell, with four burly customs officials, boarded the **LIBERTY**. None of her crew were aboard or within sight, so they cut the sloop loose from the wharf and towed her out to the 50-gun frigate **H.M.S. ROMNEY**, that had been anchored in the harbor only a few days earlier as a detriment to smugglers. Captain Connell, commander of the **ROMNEY**, had already sent a press-gang into Boston only to find another Yankee mob was there to greet them and interrupt their illegal kidnapping. He made clear his feelings to Bostonians by announcing, *"This town is a blackguard town, ruled by mobs; they have begun with me by rescuing a man whom I pressed this morning; and I will make their hearts ache before I leave."*

Hearing of the seizure of the **LIBERTY**, a Boston waterfront mob rushed down to Hancock Wharf and hurled stones at the customs officials. According to the *Boston Chronicle* of June 13, 1768, *"an angry crowd gathered, beating, stoning, and bruzing several gentlemen belonging to the Customs and Collector, mortally wounding one, and burning his boat, creating such panic that they were obliged to fly for their lives to Castle Island."* Actually, the customs comptroller, Mr. Hallowell, was not bruised at all, nor were any of the other customs officials badly hurt, but it was Hallowell's open boat that the crowd carried to Boston Common and set afire in front of John Hancock's house, Hancock being the owner of the **LIBERTY**. The only person *"mortally wounded"* during this uprising, known thereafter as *"The LIBERTY Riot,"* was James Marshall, captain of the **LIBERTY**. He suffered a heart attack and died during the heat of the riot.

John Hancock was ordered to pay 100,000 pounds sterling by the Admiralty Court, *"for smuggling and inciting a riot."* He was arrested and thrown in jail, but John Adams, his lawyer, bailed him out. Hancock wrote to an influential friend, William Reeves in London, hoping he would pass on the message to members of the British Parliament. *"Our trade is under such embarrassments and impositions,"* he wrote, *"that we have come to a resolution not to import any more goods for some time. Unless we are relieved, and these Acts repealed, we must inevitably be ruined."* At the same time, Francis Bernard, Royal Governor of Massachusetts, wrote to General Thomas Gage, commander of British military forces in America, asking for troops, for, as he said, *"Boston is being led by a trained mob."* In late September, seven British men-of-war and transport ships carrying two regiments of Redcoats and artillary, sailed single file into Boston, greeted by a fireworks display from the customs officials at Castle Island. The troops landed in Boston on October 1st, without any opposition.

The residents of Boston bristled as British soldiers swaggered down their streets, and as more British warships arrived to anchor in the harbor. The charges against the wealthy John Hancock were dropped, but his sloop **LIBERTY** was confiscated. Although her name remained the same, she was converted into a British war-sloop and sent to Newport, Rhode Island to curtail smuggling activities there. Entering Newport Harbor one cold winter morning in early 1769, she captured a Yankee brig, and the new **LIBERTY** commander accused the Yankee captain of smuggling. The Captain then called the British commander a liar and cursed him. For that afront, the commander ordered his marines to shoot the Captain. Before the marines could aim their rifles, the captain jumped overboard and made it safely to shore. That evening a flotilla of small boats out of Newport surrounded the anchored **LIBERTY** offshore, and a mob of angry Rhode Islanders boarded her. They forced the British tars and marines, including the commander, to abandon ship, then they burned the **LIBERTY** to her waterline. The enraged and embarrassed commander called their sneaky attack *"treason,"* and the British Admiralty, equally enraged, shipped off another warship to Newport.

The commander of the 4-gun schooner **H.M.S. GASPEE**, was Lieutenant William Dudingston, one of the toughest, foul-mouthed officers of the British Navy. Upon arriving at Newport, he let the residents know that he believed *"All Rhode Island sailors are smugglers,"* and if their unlawful activities continued, *"I will enjoy seeing Newport burn."* For almost two years, Dudingston successfully harassed Rhode Island's merchant mariners, stopping and seizing hundreds of vessels, cursing and insulting the captains and crews, often shipping them off to Boston for trial before the Admiralty Court. On June 9, 1772, Dudingston met his match. Captain Ben Lindsey of the little ferry-packet **HANNAH**, had plied the bay and river in a regular route from Newport to Providence to New York and back, for years. Heading up the bay toward Providence, the **GASPEE** crossed his bow, and Dudingston, through his bull-horn, ordered Captain Lindsey to *"come about, and await our boarding you for examination!"* Lindsey ignored the order and kept sailing toward Providence. Dudingston spun the **GASPEE** around and chased the **HANNAH**, intent on seizing her and severely punishing her captain. Nobody knew the waters of Narragansett Bay better than Ben Lindsey. He headed for Namquit Point, where he knew the shallow-water draft of the **HANNAH** would make it over the mud-flats at low water, but the heavier **GASPEE** would not. The **GASPEE** grounded, and with a wave of his cap to the British Navy, Captain Lindsey sailed on to Providence. Realizing that the **GASPEE** would be stuck in the mud-flats until high-tide at midnight, when Lindsey reached port he informed his fellow sea captains John Brown and Abe Whipple of Dudingston's dilemma.

A secret meeting of merchants and sea captains was held at Sabin's Tavern, Providence, early that evening. A drummer-boy was hired to march up and down the main streets of the town, announcing, *"men who wish to destroy the **GASPEE** are to meet at James Sabin's Tavern at nine o'clock."* Almost 200 men showed up at the tavern, some armed with muskets, cutlasses, and clubs. John Brown and Abe Whipple swore them all to secrecy, then they marched to Fenner's Wharf, where they piled into eight longboats. By 10 p.m., they were rowing down the river, their oars muffled with rags. When within fifty yards of the stranded **GASPEE**, a British sentry on board spotted one of the whaleboats filled with men. *"Who goes there?"* he shouted, waking Commander Dudingston, who stumbled to the slanting deck in his nightshirt. The Providence men remained silent to a man, but kept rowing steadily toward the **GASPEE**. *"Who goes there?"* Dudingston repeated, *"Speak, or we will fire on you!"* Abe Whipple, standing in the bow of the lead boat, replied, *"I am the Sheriff of Kent County, and I have a warrant to apprehend you... So surrender!"* Now Dudingston was speechless. One of the Providence men in the lead boat, Joe Bucklin, shouted to no one in particular, *"Damn it, I'm gonna shoot that fellow,"* and lifting his musket, he took aim and shot Lieutenant Dudingston in the groin. As he lay moaning on the deck, Whipple and his men boarded, and except for a few bloody noses and cracked skulls, no one was killed or wounded in the brief combat. The **GASPEE** was stripped of her valuables, and the wounded Dudingston and his crew were set adrift in a rowboat. The **GASPEE** was then torched and the Americans rowed away to the village of Pawtuxet. By dawn, as John Brown put it, *"the **GASPEE** was a heap of wet ashes."*

Dudingston recovered slowly from his wound, amidst the smiling faces of the citizens of Newport, and a King's Commission was sent from Halifax to investigate the incident, but nobody in Rhode Island would discuss the **GASPEE** attack with the commissioners. A 1000-pounds reward was issued by the British Admiralty *"for the capture of the leaders of these Rhode Island raiders,"* but nobody seemed to know who they were. Abe Whipple, on the advice of his uncle, Esek Hopkins, who later became the first Commander-in-Chief of the American Navy, took a long vacation cruise until the British in New England stopped hunting for the **GASPEE** *"raiders."*

In December of the following year, Bostonians held their famous Tea Party, and that brought General Thomas Gage to Boston as the first military governor of Massachusetts. When he came ashore from the British frigate **LIVELY**, he carried with him the *"Boston Port Bill,"* which closed the port of Boston to all commerce until the citizens paid damages for their tea party. The new Governor declared that all trade and shipping *"is henceforth transferred to Salem and Marblehead."* General Gage's flagship **LIVELY** joined the other war ships blockading the New England coast, anchoring off Marblehead. Her commander, Lieutenant William Lechmere, had orders to *"harass and impress at will, all sailors of Salem and Marblehead."* These *"press-warrents"* were issued by Vice-Admiral Graves, commander of British naval forces in America, whose headquarters was the 50-gun flagship **PRESTON**, anchored in Boston Harbor. Graves was especially angry with the people of Marblehead, for he had ordered some wax candles from a shop there and the Town Fathers had confiscated them and refused to let the admiral have them. In retaliation, Graves had Lieutenant Lechmere capture two Marblehead fishermen just outside the harbor. The fishermen were on deck of the **LIVELY**, about to become unwilling members of the British Navy, when some 100 Marbleheaders in ten whaleboats came out of the harbor and approached the British vessel. *"Keep off at your peril,"* Lechmere shouted at them. *"Deliver up our friends and we'll keep off,"* replied a Marbleheader. Lechmere ordered his marines at the gunwales to aim at the approaching boats, and the Marbleheaders aimed their muskets at Lechmere and his marines. There was a tense moment of silence as British and Yankees faced each other, prepared to fire— and this is when one of the impressed fishermen, standing helplessly on the **LIVELY** deck, leaped overboard. Lechmere tried to fire his pistol at the fisherman as the Yankees cheered, but his pistol misfired. Men in one of the whaleboats hauled their friend aboard, and quickly started rowing him back into the harbor. The British, however, caught the second fisherman before he could jump, chained him and escorted him below deck of the **LIVELY**. It was a standoff, both sides slowly retreating, each getting only half of what they wanted. Vice Admiral Graves was furious when he heard that ruffians in rowboats had dared to challenge the commander of one of His Majesty's flagships. He warned the Town Fathers of Marblehead that he would retaliate with harsh measures. The few Town Fathers with Tory tendencies decided it might be wise to be nice to the Vice-Admiral, so they sent him his delayed candles with a letter of apology, agreeing *"to* *pay all costs and damages, and promise in the future there never shall be any cause of complaint."*

    Vice-Admiral Graves and General Gage, respectively commanding the Navy and Army in America, both stationed in Boston, detested each other. Their fathers also had been enemies. This riff between admiral and general filtered down through the ranks, causing constant friction between British soldiers and sailors, which worked to the advantage of the rebellious Yankees. Often, when the Admiral received orders from London concerning troop movements, or General Gage received orders from Parliament, in which the fleet was involved, heated arguments between Graves and Gage ensued, many times within ear-shot of their men. A top-secret communication to Graves from Parliament, which he received in October of 1774, when passed on to General Gage, caused the inevitable ruckus between the two leaders. The order called for the prohibition of all gunpowder deliveries from any source to the American Colonies. General Gage made it known to his friends that he didn't think the Vice-Admiral was intelligent enough or capable of stopping the delivery of powder into New England. The Vice-Admiral, hearing of the General's off-handed comments, was furious, and due to their feuding, the Americans learned of this top-secret order, placing a new and devistating restriction on their need and desire to defend themselves.

    General Gage lived, without invitation, in the home of the Shaws, a large anti-British family of Boston. Their neighbor was Paul Revere, a member of the clandestine *"Committee of Safety."* Soon after the restriction on powder was revealed, Revere got word from the Shaws that the General had met further resistance from Graves when he demanded that the Admiral's men-of-war accompany transports with two regiments of soldiers to Fort William And Mary in Portsmouth, New Hampshire to protect the British powder, arms, and ammunition that were stored there under guard of only a few soldiers. While Vice-Admiral Graves sputtered and fumed over the general's order, Paul Revere was on his horse, galloping the 60 miles over icy roads to Durham, New Hampshire. He arrived at the home of *"Committee of Safety"* leader John Sullivan in mid-afternoon of December 13th. As Revere and his horse relaxed after the long ride, Sullivan sent word to some forty men in Portsmouth to meet at his home in Durham early that evening and to come armed. Under the cloak of darkness, Sullivan led his men, now swelled to well over 200, to a lumbering old sailboat, called a gundalow, docked in the Pisataqua River. In the gundalow and in accompanying barges, they silently sailed and rowed down river a few miles, and landed in the mud-flats off Fort William And Mary. Then, they waded and sloshed ashore. Standing outside the walls of the fort, Sullivan shouted to one Captain Corcoran, who commanded the fort, to leave with his men and they wouldn't be hurt. *"I immediately ordered three four-pounders to be fired at them and then small arms,"* Corcoran later reported, but he didn't aim his cannons or muskets at anyone, so no one was hurt. He then surrendered the fort. *"We were stormed on all quarters,"* was Corcoran's excuse for surrender.

Throughout most of the night, as the tide rose, Sullivan and his men carried arms and powder from the fort through waist-deep icy water to the gundalow and barges—97 heavy kegs of powder and 100 muskets in all— then they sailed away. Most of this valuable loot was hidden under the pulpit of the Durham meeting house, safely stashed away for future use. Gage blamed Graves and Graves blamed Gage for allowing this disgrace and plundering of a British fort. The angriest of all, however, was King George III, who, it was said, *"never was more furious than he was after the raid on Fort William And Mary."* The King demanded of both Vice-Admiral Graves and General Gage that the culprits be seized and severely punished, but nobody seemed to know who these marauding thieves were. The powder was put to good use a few months later at the Battle of Bunker Hill.

Since everyone who came into and left Boston town had to get a pass from the British authorities, General Gage was suspicious of the energetic traveler Paul Revere, who had obtained a pass to leave Boston for Portsmouth on the day of the raid on the fort. Paul realized the British were keeping an eye on him, therefore, when given orders by Joseph Warren, leader of the Massachusetts Committee of Safety, on the evening of April 18, 1775, *"to alert every village and farm"* of British troop movements, Paul used a rowboat to get out of Boston. He rowed, muffling his oars with his wife's petticoat, to Charlestown, right past the anchored man-of-war **H. M. S. SOMERSET**. In Charlestown, he procured a horse, then galloped off on the lantern signal from the old North Church, *"one if by land and two if by sea."* Although there were two lanterns in the church steeple, the British troops didn't move by sea, but merely crossed the Charles River in rowboats to Cambridge. Thanks to Paul and a few others, the villagers and farmers got the message— next morning came *"the shot heard 'round the world."*

Since the only way to get information out of America to Europe was by sea, Joseph Warren had a salty counterpart for Paul Revere to deliver important messages abroad. He was John Derby of Salem, Massachusetts. Nine days after the Battle of Lexington and Concord,

Warren sent Derby on a secret speedy mission to England in his 62-ton schooner **QUERO**. In the dead of the night, the **QUERO** slipped out of Salem, snuck by the **LIVELY** anchored outside the harbor, and raced for England. Derby arrived in London on May 28th, and delivered a packet of letters and newspaper clippings to Arthur Lee, an American sympathizer. Joseph Warren's letter to Lee read, in part, *"we most ardently wish that the papers herewith enclosed may be immediately printed and dispatched through every town in England."* The newspaper clippings that Derby had delivered, and Warren wanted reprinted in every English newspaper, were copies of the four-page weekly *Essex Gazette*, published in Salem. The four pages were devoted to what happened at Lexington and Concord, from the American point of view, and depicted General Gage and his British troops as cruel war-mongers. Derby and Lee delivered their papers throughout England. The King and the English lords were in near-panic when this first news of the battle appeared in print for all Britain to read. Up to this time, the King and Parliament had carefully controlled all information on troubles in America, informing the English people that the various prior incidents in New England had been merely rabel-rousings by waterfront ruffians. The information on Lexington and Concord from the *Essex Gazette* shocked the British causing the London stock-exchange to plummet.

Lord Dartmouth immediately dispatched a letter to General Gage: *"The **QUERO** was sent by the enemies of this government on purpose to make an impression here,"* he told Gage. *"They represented the Affair between the King's Troops and the Rebel Provincials in a light most favorable to their own views, conveying every possible prejudice and misrepresentation of the truth. Their industry in this occassion had its effect in leaving for some days a false impression upon peoples minds."* Gage had, in fact, sent his *"official version of the battles"* in the **H. M. S. SUKEY**, which left Boston four days before the **QUERO** left Salem, but didn't arrive in England until nine days after Derby had delivered his newspapers. Lord Dartmouth demanded that Derby come before him to explain his treasonous act, *"upon penalty of imprisonment,"* but Derby, quickly and quietly, boarded the **QUERO** and headed back for New England. When he arrived home, the Provincial Congress offered to pay him for his voyage, but he replied, *"the success of my mission is sufficient reward."*

While Derby was on his newspaper route, the Committees of Safety in Connecticut and Massachusetts, realizing that Vermont's Lake Region had to be controlled or the British would swoop down on the New England Colonies from the North, sent volunteers to Castletown.

The rough and tumble Ethan Allen and aristocratic Benedict Arnold, both Connecticut boys, met with their two small armies on the banks of Lake Champlain. Their missions from the two Committees of Safety were the same; attack the British held forts at Ticonderoga and at Crown Point, but they needed boats to ferry them to the New York side of the lake. *"Two old scows"* were stolen from Tories at Bridport and taken to Hand Cove in Vermont, where the troops departed, having to make two trips across to carry the Green Mountain Boys and then Arnold's militiamen. To Arnold's chargrin, Allen took Ticonderoga before he got there, without a casualty, and the Vermont *"boys"* then took Crown Point. In order to hold the lake, Allen and Arnold knew they needed ships as well as the two forts.

"A party of thirty men under Captain Sam Herrick of Massachusetts," was sent to Skanesborough, now Whitehall, New York, from Castletown to attack Tory Major Philip Skene's troops and to confiscate Skene's 40-ton, six-gun schooner **LIBERTY** at anchor there. Herrick, under Arnold's orders, easily took the village and the schooner on May 9th, 1775. Five days later Benedict Arnold with 50 men showed up and boarded the **LIBERTY**. He sailed her up the lake and into the Richelieu River, intent on a surprise attack of the British garrison at St. John's. Ethan Allen and his men followed in a flotilla of small sailing boats, hoping to attack St. John's before Arnold did. Arnold got there first, landing his men close to the British barracks. The Redcoats immediately *"dropped their arms and surrendered,"* Arnold later reported to the Massachusetts Committee of Safety. Then 17 of Arnold's men attacked the 50-ton sloop **GEORGE** that was anchored close by. *"We took a sergeant and his party of twelve men, and the King's sloop,"* Arnold reported, *"without loss on either side."* Aboard the **GEORGE**, which Arnold renamed **ENTERPRISE**, his men confiscated *"two six-pounder cannons, mortars, muskets, and sterling silver."* The **ENTERPRISE**, on her way back to the lake, met up with Allen and his men sailing up the river. The Green Moutain Boys were upset that they had missed all the fun. An on going feud, much like that between Graves and Gage developed between Arnold and Allen. Most important, however, it was through both their efforts that the rebels now controlled New England's largest lake.

Britania, however, still ruled the waves off the coast of America, but one little incident, three days after the **LIBERTY** was captured at Skanesborough, should have warned the British Navy that their constant taking of liberties might some day turn the tide on the high seas. On May 12, at Buzzard's Bay, Cape Cod, the British sloop **H.M.S.**

FALCON, accosted a small merchant vessel coming into the village of Dartmouth from the West Indies. British Commander John Linzee placed tars and marines aboard the merchantman, and his tender took her in tow, destined for British headquarters in Boston. Rounding the Cape, the British were met by a flotilla of little sailboats, all manned by citizens of Dartmouth. After a brief skirmish, the British surrendered, giving up their merchantman prize and the FALCON's tender as well. The Dartmouth sailors took 14 British marines to Cambridge as prisoners-of-war. This daring sea exploit by the villagers of Dartmouth is referred to by some historians as "the first naval action of the Revolution." Be it the first naval action or not, it should have hinted to the British that they were more vulnerable on the sea than they thought — the cause of liberty providing men with great inner strength. In 1775, it became the equalizer, cutting the British Goliath down to size. The Rebels in their sailboats and old scows were soon slinging pebbles that would finally strike Vice-Admiral Graves right between the eyes.

The sloop UNITY defeats the British schooner MARGARETTA (renamed MACHIAS LIBERTY) at Machiasport, Maine, on June 12, 1775. Many historians consider this battle to be "the first naval engagement of the Revolutionary War." - Painting by Robert Lambdin, courtesy of the Machiasport Historical Society.

II
WASHINGTON'S WET AND WILD WARRIORS

At age fifteen he was a midshipman in His Majesty's Navy, but he never went to sea. His father had died when he was a boy, and his older brother, Lawrence, a naval officer, ran the family of seven children from that day on. He urged George to enlist in the navy, but his mother was opposed. With his gear stashed aboard the ship that was to take him on his first cruise, George Washington was about to leave home. His mother cried and pleaded with him not to go as his older brother insisted that he leave for the waiting ship. A Mother's tears won the day and changed American history. George went to the ship, but only to get his gear and return his midshipman's uniform. When he was older he joined the army, and on July 3, 1775 he rode into Cambridge, Massachusetts as Commander-in-Chief of America's Continental Army. George, however, was aware that the king's forces had to be defeated at sea as well as on land, and his first endeavor was meeting the great war-ships of the British Navy with rowboats and little sailboats.

Even before Washington arrived at Cambridge, 15 days after the Battle of Bunker-Hill, there had been two sea battles between British forces and American Minutemen. The first was at Romney Marsh, a section of Chelsea, Massachusetts, now Revere, on May 27, 1775, and the second was at Machias, Maine on June 3, 1775. Since these battles occurred after the Battle of Lexington and Concord, both communities claim to be The Birthplace Of The American Navy.

The *"Battle of Chelsea Creek,"* as it is called, began as a simple raiding expedition for food from the American army camp at Cambridge by Colonel John Stark with some 300 New Hampshire and Massachusetts Militiamen. Under cover of darkness, they made their way through the tall marsh grass, waited until ebb-tide and waded across in waist-deep water to Hog Island, and thence to Noodle Island, where the British troops of Boston allowed sheep and cattle to graze before being slaughtered. Stark and his men intended to drive the sheep and cattle across the shallows from island to island and then to Cambridge, where the Rebel troops were camped and in need of fresh meat. The cows, bulls, sheep and lambs had been confiscated from farms along the New England coast by crews of British men-of-war, and dropped off at Noodle Island; therefore, the Americans felt no qualms about stealing them back. What they didn't expect was that they'd get caught in the midst of their cattle rustling. The British had stationed some 200 Redcoats at a point overlooking Noodle Island, apparently expecting just such a raid.

When the alarm was sounded, a British sloop-of-war and a schooner, towing eleven barges filled with some 400 British regulars, were immediately on the scene, sailing down Chelsea Creek. Some of the barges landed at Noodle Island as the Americans tried to retreat back to Hog Island with hundreds of sheep and cattle. *"A heavy fire was opened from the sloop and schooner,"* General William Sumner later reported, *"under cover of which, the British marines advanced on our men."* The schooner carried 16 cannons, the sloop, 8 cannons, and each barge had a swivel-gun mounted on the bow — the Americans had only muskets.

The militiamen *"reserved their fire until sure of aim,"* Sumner tells us. The result was disasterous for the advancing British marines; over 100 killed and many wounded, but not one American received a scratch. The militiamen then quickly waded across to Hog Island with the sheep and cattle, *"the regulars who remained upon Noodle's Island, firing upon them very briskly by platoons."* The barges, sloop and schooner, however, cut off their retreat to the mainland, and Stark had to send a swimmer-runner to Cambridge, asking General Putnam for reinforcements. Not only did Putnam send 300 men and two four-pounder cannons, but he came himself— *"Old Put"* was not one to miss a swipe at the British. When he arrived at Chelsea Neck, he waded out into the water and hailed the commander of the British schooner. *"Do you surrender?"* he shouted. The British lieutenant laughed and replied with two shots from his deck cannons. *"Old Put"* had his two cannons hidden in the marshgrass, and he let the schooner have both barrels. The schooner was in shallow water and was having trouble manuevering. The American Minutemen took advantage of this, wading out with General Putnam. *"A heavy fire ensued on both sides for two hours,"* wrote Sumner. *"The armed sloop and a great number of boats came to the aid of the schooner."* Finally, this bizarre naval battle of a British armed schooner and a sloop-of-war against Minutemen wading waist-deep in a tidal-river, came to an end. The sloop, *"under hot fire,"* was forced to retreat and the men in the schooner, on order from their commander, abandoned ship. The Minutemen boarded her, took everything that wasn't nailed down, and torched her. By this time, Stark and his men had escaped to the mainland from Hog Island with some 400 sheep and 200 head of cattle. By dawn, the *"Battle Of Chelsea Creek"* was over, and there was no doubt as to which side was victorious. Yet when civilians, mostly children from nearby villages and towns, came down to the waters edge in the morning to view the smouldering remains of the British schooner, the British man-of-war **SOMERSET** sailed in, and with 68 cannons, bombarded them, miraculously not killing any of the spectators, but wounding a woman and three children.

The next day, Lieutenant James Moore, of the **H.M.S. MARGARETTA** got his orders from Vice-Admiral Samuel Graves at Boston to escort the 90-ton sloop **UNITY** and the schooner **POLLY** carrying foodstuffs to Machias, Maine. He was to wait for Ichabod Jones, a British sympathizer, to unload the food and reload with lumber needed to build British army barracks in Boston. The convoy arrived at Machias on June 2nd, but Lieutenant Moore wouldn't allow the barrels of pork and flour to be unloaded from the **UNITY** and **POLLY** to feed the 100 near starving Machias families, unless they all agreed to allow Ichabod Jones to continue trading with the British Army. The villagers, as isolated as they were on the northern Maine coast, had only recently received news of the Battle of Lexington and Concord. As they met to decide on Lieutenant Moore's terms, Ichabod Jones' business partner, Benjamin Foster, called for another meeting of the more rebellious woodsmen at Job Burnham's Tavern. The men in the tavern decided they would kidnap Jones and Lieutenant Moore and steal their vessels.

June 11th was a Sunday, and what better day to capture British officers than when they were congregated together in church. The Machias Minutemen crossed the river that morning in small boats with the intent of surrounding the church where Jones and Moore were attending services, but a servant warned Jones that they were coming. Ichabod bolted out the back door of the church and headed for the woods to hide. Lieutenant Moore and his second officer, jumped out the church window and outraced the Minutemen to the **MARGARETTA**'s tender that was tied up at dockside. They escaped down river and into the harbor where their warship was at anchor.

Ichabod was soon discovered cowering in the woods. Lieutenant Moore sent a message ashore to Foster and his men: *"I will protect Mr. Jones with my life, and if his vessels are burned, I will destroy Machias."* The Machias Minutemen didn't burn either of Jones' vessels, but they did take them over. Ben Foster commanded the **POLLY** and rebel leader Jeremiah O'Brien took over the **UNITY**. Together, they decided to go after the **MARGARETTA**. Lieutenant Moore in his slow moving yet heavily armed vessel, decided to head for Boston, but O'Brien, with 40 men armed with muskets, axes, swords and pitchforks, caught up with him in the **UNITY** before he could get out of the harbor. *"Surrender to America, or I'll fire on you,"* shouted O'Brien to Lt. Moore. *"Fire and be damned,"* replied Moore. The **MARGARETTA** fired at the **UNITY** and **POLLY** as they approached; one to starboard, one to port. O'Brien brought the **UNITY** alongside in an attempt to have his men board the **MARGARETTA**. Lieutenant Moore heaved grenades onto the **UNITY** deck, but O'Brien and his men dodged them and remained unscathed. John O'Brien, Jeremiah's brother, was first to leap onto the **MARGARETTA**'s barricaded deck, but the tip of a British sword forced him to leap overboard again. He was picked up by the **UNITY** crew, and Jeremiah headed the **UNITY** back in, this time causing her bowsprit to tear through the **MARGARETTA**'s mainsail. The Machias Minutemen leaped aboard, fighting British marines in hand-to-hand combat.

Lieutenant Moore received, *"two balls, one in his right breast, another in his belly,"* and his second officer was severely wounded. Without leaders, the British surrendered. Moore later died of his wounds. One British marine was killed and four wounded. Of the Americans, two were killed and five were wounded. The **MARGARETTA** was towed back into Machias, *"in great triumph, with colors flying."* The Minutemen renamed her **MACHIAS LIBERTY**. The captured British sailors and marines, with Ichabod Jones, were marched off under guard to Cambridge, arriving there about the same time George Washington did.

Vice-Admiral Graves was furious at the capture of the **MARGARETTA** and the lumber vessels— the British were in desperate need of lumber to build barracks. *"Take the H. M. Schooner HOPE, under Lieutenant Dawson,"* he directed his nephew Captain John Graves, *"and proceed together to Maine in search of these Machias Pirates, whom you are to do your utmost to take, sink, burn, or destroy by all means in your power."* Accompanying the **HOPE** was the schooner **DILIGENT** which O'Brien and Ben Foster, in the **MACHIAS LIBERTY**, soon overtook and captured off the coast of Maine. George Washington, urging O'Brien to continue his privateering along the Maine Coast, shipped 50 men and a supply of food to Machias to protect and feed this isolated but active outpost. O'Brien kept the **DILIGENT** as his flagship, and by mid-July, 1775 his small fleet had captured five more British vessels. At about the same time, Washington wrote Congress that, *"each Colony should defend their own seacoast at their own expense."* The Massachusetts Provincial Congress complied on August 23, 1775, commissioning O'Brien *"Commander of the armed schooner DILIGENT and the sloop MACHIAS LIBERTY, for the purpose of guarding the sea coast."*

The British, controlling the high seas from bases in Halifax and Boston, were supplied almost daily with provisions and ammunition from Great Britain. The American Army of 14,500 untrained militiamen at Cambridge was in constant need of provisions, and the only way to get them, Washington concluded, was to steal from the British. He prompted the leaders of Massachusetts, Rhode Island, Connecticut and New Hampshire to outfit privateers to intercept British supply-ships. Washington asked Rhode Islanders to send vessels to Bermuda to confiscate British gunpowder that was warehoused there. The sloop **KATY** was sent to Bermuda by the Governor of Rhode Island and succeeded in her mission, but Governor Cooke and his assemblymen could not afford men or money to create a navy for Washington. George would have to rely on the sailors and fishermen in his ragtag Army to prey on the merchantships of the British Navy. The General's only available vessels were whaleboats, called *"row-galleys,"* small fishing sloops and schooners — and they were in short supply.

At Penobscot, Maine, Colonel James Cargill with some 300 Mainiac fishermen in 14 to 20-foot whaleboats, managed to capture five British supply ships before the Revolution was four months old. Cargill often hid his boats close to shore or behind islands near the British trade route from Halifax to Boston, sometimes camouflaging them with pine branches. As merchant vessels passed by, he and his men would quickly row out and surround them with ten to twenty whaleboats, armed with bow guns. More times than not, the British merchant captain would surrender his ship and cargo without a fight. In one instance, Cargill and his crew captured a detachment of British marines and sailors on an island in the process of collecting firewood and hunting wild animals for the troops in Boston. After rounding up the foraging Redcoats, Cargill seized their vessel.

On the night of July 11, 1775, Washington sent Ben Tupper of Sharon, Massachusetts on a whaleboat expedition to destroy the British stronghold at Castle Island in Boston Harbor. With muffled oars, 300 men in twenty boats rowed around the British warships in the harbor and quietly landed on the island. They rounded up 100 sheep and 30 cows and loaded them into their boats. Then they set every building on the island, but the lighthouse, afire. A small detachment of Redcoats sent to the island put up slight resistance, and 16 of them were captured by Tupper's men. An estimated 12 British soldiers were killed or wounded, but only one American was killed. With their booty of beasts and British prisoners, Tupper and his men made it safely back to the mainland. About two weeks later, after the British had begun rebuilding their fortifications and supply depot at Castle Island, the whaleboat crews returned for another night raid. This time, instead of cows and sheep, they confiscated boats and gunpowder. Then they torched the new buildings, this time including the island lighthouse. As they rowed back to the mainland, they were spotted and chased by the **H. M. S. PRESTON**. The whaleboats scattered, but the **PRESTON** managed to destroy one whaleboat with a cannonball, wounding two Americans. The others escaped unscathed.

Like a swarm of pesty mosquitoes, whaleboaters under Ben Tupper returned to Castle Island to harrass the British again on July 31st. British carpenters had just completed construction of a new lighthouse, and the island was now heavily guarded by British regulars. Tupper and his men landed at dawn. The British had been up late the night before celebrating the completion of the new lighthouse when Tupper surprised them. Many Redcoats were killed or wounded in the attack and 23 were taken prisoner. Only one American was killed in the skirmish. Again, all the newly constructed buildings, including the lighthouse, were burned to the ground, and the Americans rowed off with the lighthouse lamp— a precious beacon for British supply ships coming in at night from England and Halifax. As the whaleboats headed for Hull, the **H. M. S. LIVELY** and **H. M. S. PRESTON** pursued them. A one hour sea battle ensued, the **PRESTON** destroying one whaleboat, killing one sailor and wounding four. Tupper's crew managed to hit a British longboat from the **PRESTON**, killing six British marines. The commander of **H. M. S. LIVELY** was also killed, but not in battle. In his haste to board the **LIVELY** in pursuit of the American whaleboats, Commander Colthurst fell off the island dock, struck his head, and died of the injury.

In some of their raids, Tupper and his men successfully completed their missions without any resistance at all. Rowing from Hingham, under the noses of the British anchored in their warships at Nantasket Road, the whaleboats landed at Nantasket. The crews loaded 70 cartloads of grain into the boats and rowed back to Hingham without being spotted— the British were about to confiscate the grain for their troops in Boston, but Tupper had beat them to it. Probably the most successful of Ben Tupper's raids was off the island of Martha's Vineyard where two merchant vessels were anchored and filled with cargo for the British in Boston. Tupper and his men surrounded the vessels and were about to board, when the Tory seamen surrendered. The food and war materials were sent to Cambridge, and the vessels became part of Washington's little but ever increasing navy. The **HARRISON** and **HESTER** were refitted as war ships for America, one to be commanded by Ben Tupper himself.

The British cargo-ship **FRIENDS** of London, carrying materials and weapons for the British troops in Boston came into what her Captain

Bowie thought was Boston Harbor on January 15, 1776. Three whaleboats with armed men aboard came out from shore to greet her. Captain Offin Boardman came along side the **FRIENDS** in one of the whaleboats. *"Is this Boston?"* Captain Bowie shouted down to Boardman. *"It is,"* replied Boardman, *"and I am the Boston pilot, directed to bring you in."* Boardman and 17 of his men were then welcomed aboard the **FRIENDS** by the Englishmen. *"Strike your British flag!"* was Boardman's first order once on deck. Captain Bowie was astonished, but he and his men surrendered gracefully to the whaleboat crews. *"A terrible mistake on your part,"* Boardman smiled as he explained to Bowie that he had come into Newburyport, Massachusetts, not Boston, and that the **FRIENDS** was a prize of war.

Harassing the British Navy with rowboats wasn't enough for Washington. He had a wild and almost unmanagable regiment of soldiers camped at Cambridge, and every one of them was from Marblehead, Massachusetts. In a tactful move to rid the army camp of the mischevious fishermen, and at the same time create an American sailing navy, he dubbed the Marbleheaders his *"Amphibious Regiment,"* under the command of Marbleheader Colonel John Glover, and had the most troublesome of the lot, 36 in number, march themselves back to their home town. In Marblehead, diarist Ashly Bowen wrote in his Day Book, *"August 24, 1775. Came to towne a company of vollunteers from the camp at Cambreedg, in Order for a cruse in Glover's schooner."* On September 5, Ashly wrote, *"Sailed on an unknown experdishon, a schooner of Capt. John Glover's, Nick Broughton, Captain of Marines and John Gail, master of schooner."*

John Glover's little 45-ton fishing schooner **HANNAH** is considered the first official ship of the American Navy. John, who later became one of Washington's most acclaimed generals, owned a wharf and fishing business across the wide mouth of Salem Harbor from Marblehead at Beverly, Massachusetts. It was from this wharf that the **HANNAH** departed on her first official mission on September 5th, with 36 men and three officers after being refitted as a warship at Beverly. The **HANNAH** was built at Salisbury, Massachusetts, but her home port had been Marblehead, and everyone who sailed aboard her on that first naval voyage was from Marblehead. Thus, an ongoing feud exists to this day between the people of Marblehead and Beverly who both claim their community as *"The Birthplace of the American Navy."*

George Washington's orders to **HANNAH**'s commander, Nicholson Broughton, were quite explicit: *"September 2, 1775 — You, being appointed a Captain in the Army of the United Colonies, are* *hereby directed to take Command of a detachment of said Army and proceed on board the schooner **HANNAH** at Beverly, lately fitted out and equipped with arms, ammunition and provisions at Continental expense... You are to search out and seize such vessels as may be found on the High Seas or elsewhere, bound inward or outward to or from Boston, in the service of the Ministerial Army."*

Only a few hours out to sea, the **HANNAH** was chased into Gloucester Harbor by the **H. M. S. LIVELY**. Broughton waited inside the harbor until he thought the coast was clear and next day sailed out again. Seven hours later he records in his log, *"I saw a large ship and hailed her. She was from Piscataqua, (New Hampshire) bound for Boston. I told the captain to go into Cape Ann, he being very loth, I told him if he did not, I would fire on her, and he went into Cape Ann..."* She was the 260-ton brig **UNITY**, loaded with lumber and naval supplies. He turned over his first prize vessel, her cargo and crew to the Gloucester Minutemen, who would transfer all goods and prisoners to Cambridge. The **HANNAH** crew was ecstatic, for Washington had promised that they would each receive a share in one-third the profit from the cargo of every vessel they brought in. Hearing of the capture, however, George Washington announced that the **UNITY** was not an enemy vessel and her cargo was not being delivered by Tories to the British. The vessel was owned by Portsmouth's John Langdon, a delegate to America's Continental Congress — a patriot whom the British had sworn to hang if captured. Washington ordered that the **UNITY** be released, her cargo returned, and her captain and crew receive an apology from Nick Broughton.

Feeling victimized by George Washington's wrath, and angry at not receiving prize money, the **HANNAH** crew, all 36 of them, mutinied. They left the schooner at Gloucester, called their Captain Broughton a few unflattering names, and refused to sail again with him. Washington had them arrested by the Gloucester Militia, and at gunpoint, marched to Army Headquarters in Cambridge. A few days later they were court-martialed and found guilty of *"mutiny, riot and disobedience to orders."* Their leader, Joseph Searle, was given 39 lashes of the whip and was kicked out of the American Army. Ten others of the Marblehead mutineers were drummed out of military service, but 25 of them were repreaved. A new crew of *"volunteers"* from Glover's Amphibious Regiment were selected as crewmen for Captain Broughton, and on September 29th, the **HANNAH** set sail once again.

Obviously George Washington was unnerved by the **HANNAH** mutiny, but he still had undying faith in the little navy he had created.

His enthusiasm, in fact, may have prompted him to tell his first lie, for on October 13, 1775, he wrote to his brother John that, *"I have fitted out several privateers, with soldiers, who have been bred to the sea, and have no doubt of making captures of several British transports, some of which have already fallen into our hands, laden with provisions. . ."*. The fact of the matter was, that by mid-October Washington had fitted out only one vessel, the **HANNAH**, and her only capture had been the **UNITY**. It was rumored that, since his youthful folly of chopping down the cherry-tree, George Washington had never told a lie, but if so, he was certainly stretching the truth about his little navy to his brother John. Three days before this letter was written the **HANNAH** was attacked by a British man-of-war, and George Washington really had no navy at all. The only American vessels that provided any battle achievements of note from September to mid-October, 1775, was the **DILIGENT** and **MACHIAS LIBERTY** of Maine, who were not sponsored by Washington, but by Massachusetts. The **DILIGENT**, commanded by Captain Stephen Smith, and the **MACHIAS LIBERTY**, under Jeremiah O'Brien, successfully attacked and defeated the occupants of a British fort at the mouth of Canada's St. John's River in mid-September, and the **DILIGENT** captured a British brig, the **LORD BRITON**, carrying cattle, sheep, arms and ammunition.

The British, it seems, had a deep fear of Jeremiah O'Brien's little fleet. O'Brien was called *"The Machias Admiral"* by the Colonials, and Vice-Admiral Graves was determined to crush him and his supporters. Graves ordered the commanders of His Majesty's warships; **CANCEAUX, HALIFAX, SPITFIRE** and **SYMMETRY** to *"destroy all shipping in the harbors of Marblehead, Salem, Newburyport, Gloucester, Portsmouth, and all ports in Maine, and make a most vigorous effort to burn the Towns. First, burn Gloucester. . ."* This impressive fleet of British warships arrived at Gloucester just as the **HANNAH**, with her new crew, was sailing out of port. According to Broughton, the **CANCEAUX**, commanded by Henry Mowat, with intent to burn Gloucester, *"was chased away by the HANNAH,"*. Mowat had thought that the **HANNAH** was O'Brien's ship **DILIGENT**. Yet, Captain Mowat states in a report to Vice-Admiral Graves that, *"It was not with reluctance I passed this port(* Gloucester*) as your orders directed me there first, but a storm prevented our ships from entering the Harbor."* Commander Mowat sailed on to Falmouth (now Portland, Maine) and burned the town to the ground with red-hot cannonballs, telling the inhabitants before he started firing that, *"you are guilty of the most unpardonable Rebelion."* Mowat, however, never attacked the other towns on the Vice-Admiral's list, and he feared even going near Machias.

On September 14th, Graves received a dispatch from General Gage, which in part read, *"I have intelligence which I depend upon, of the Rebels fitting out Cruisers to intercept our supplies, and to seize our dispatches from Europe."* The only active cruiser at the time was the **HANNAH**, and the Vice-Admiral sent the 16-gun, 316-ton sloop **NAUTILUS**, Captain John Collins commanding, to seek her out and destroy her. The **NAUTILUS** met up with the **HANNAH** as she sailed from Gloucester to Beverly on the afternoon of October 10th, and immediately gave chase. Nick Broughton headed hell-bent into Beverly Harbor, where sand and mud banks made the manuevering of large sailing ships difficult, and where recently erected fortifications flanked the harbor mouth at Beverly and neighboring Salem. In her haste to make Glover Wharf, however, the **HANNAH** grounded on a sandbank. The **NAUTILUS**, with 125 British sailors and marines aboard, followed her in. Confident of an easy kill, Captain Collins anchored in the shallows nearby. The **HANNAH** *"was aground very near the beach,"* Collins later reported to Vice-Admiral Graves. *"I thought it best to endeavor setting her on fire, and immediately hoisted out the boats, and got combustibles ready for that purpose — I continued firing a number of shots at her."* Broughton and his crew, with cannonballs whizzing around them, began stripping the **HANNAH** of her weapons and other valuables. Then they all jumped overboard and waded ashore. The **NAUTILUS** cannoneers were not good marksmen, and many of their shots went astray, some of them falling into Beverly town and catching a barn and stable on fire. The Beverly and Salem Militia were alerted and rushed to their battle stations. Broughton and his men fired at the **NAUTILUS** with their muskets, doing little damage, but once the local militiamen were on the scene, the **NAUTILUS** was caught in a crossfire from Beverly and Salem. From the Salem side, cannonballs from Fort Lee started finding the mark, and in trying to manuever his sloop away from the cannon fire, the **NAUTILUS**, like the **HANNAH**, grounded on a sandbar. Hiding behind boulders on the beach, Beverly marksmen forced the boats from the **NAUTILUS** to turn back to their ship, before they were able to row to the **HANNAH** and torch her. The tide was going out and both vessels were soon high and dry and under heavy fire. This sea battle between naval warships, is considered by many historians as the first official battle of the American Navy, yet, during the battle, neither ship was afloat. After hours of raining cannonballs and stinging musketfire, the rigging and sails of the **NAUTILUS** were tattered and torn. The **HANNAH**, however, had little damage done to her. Captain Collins had no alternative than to stay and take a beating until the tide turned and he could sail his sloop off the sandbar. It was after dark before he managed to do this, and the **NAUTILUS** limped away out of the harbor at about 8 p.m. One British tar had been killed and another lost his leg. Salem's David Newall had his hand blown off while firing a cannon at Fort Lee, and this was the extent of the casualties. If nothing more, the Americans had humiliated a British warship, but it was the last and only Hurrah for the **HANNAH**. Because she was too small and sailed too slow, Washington decided to replace her with four larger schooners from Marblehead. The **HANCOCK, FRANKLIN, LEE,** and **WARREN**, considered the 2nd, 3rd, 4th, and 5th warships of the American Navy, were leased from their owners by Washington at a cost of four shillings per ton per month.

The 72-ton fishing schooner **SPEEDWELL** of Marblehead, was sailed across the bay to Beverly where she was fitted out as the battle cruiser **HANCOCK**. Her commander was Nick Broughton, the old commander of the **HANNAH**. She took on 75 crewmen from Glover's regiment, and set sail for Canadian waters on October 22nd with the 60-ton **FRANKLIN**, a former Marblehead fishing schooner, with commander Archibald Selman and 75 Marblehead mariners aboard. Washington's orders to them were to *"seize two north country brigantines and other transports laden with arms, men, or stores. If you miss them, cruise to the mouth of the St. Lawrence River, but Canadian vessels, not in the British military service are not to be seized."*

Broughton and Selman couldn't find the brigantines carrying arms and ammunition that Washington wanted so badly, but they did seize, without much resistance, seven minor transports at the mouth of the St. Lawrence, most of them carrying fish and firewood. Sailing to Prince Edward Island, they attacked the capitol of Charlottetown, suspecting that British recruits were being trained there, but they were wrong. To compensate for their folly, they kidnapped three civilians, the Attorney General of Canada and two island councilors. They delivered their meager booty and three prisoners to Washington's headquarters in Cambridge. George was surprised, but not pleasingly so— he had no quarrel with the people of Prince Edward Island, then called St. John's, and hoped to neutralize them. He immediately released Broughton's and Selman's prisoners, returned the property that was taken from them, and personally saw to it that the captive dignitaries were safely shipped back to their island. He then called Broughton and Selman before him and gave them a tongue-lashing. Stephen Moylan, Washington's secretary tells us that, *"Broughton and Selman are indolant and inactive souls. Their time was out yesterday, and from frequent rubs they got from me, they feel sore, and decline serving longer."*

Exactly one week after the **HANCOCK** and **FRANKLIN** sailed north from Beverly, the 74-ton schooner **LEE**, formerly **TWO BROTHERS** of Marblehead, and the 64-ton **WARREN**, formerly the **HAWK** of Marblehead, sailed out of Beverly as refitted battle cruisers in Washington's Navy. The **LEE**, carrying 14 cannons, was commanded by John Manley of Marblehead, and boasted a 50 man Marblehead crew, but the **WARREN**, commanded by Winborn Adams of Portsmouth, was manned by 50 New Hampshire men. Two days out to sea, the **LEE** captured her first prize off Cape Ann, but she was a 40-ton American merchant schooner coming from Ireland, and Washington ordered that she be released, which almost caused another mutiny of a Marblehead crew. *"Our rascally privateersmen go on at the old rate,"* Washington wrote General Reed on November 20, *"mutinying if they cannot do as they please... They have done nothing worth mentioning in the prize way..."* With the ink still wet on Washington's pen, the former **TWO BROTHERS** captured the 80-ton schooner **TWO SISTERS**, carrying meat and butter from Ireland to the troops in Boston. A few days later Manley and his crew took the merchantman **NORTH BRITON**, and both prizes were sent into Beverly. Seven days after Washington wrote his discouraging letter to General Reed, Captain Manley captured the British brig **NANCY** carrying 2,000 muskets, 100,000 flints, 30,000 round-shot, many barrels of gunpowder, and the greatest prize of all, a 2,700-pound 13-inch brass mortar. Congress decreed that *"it is the noblest piece of ordinance ever landed in America,"* and they congratulated Manley, who had taken this *"floating arsenal"* without a fight. The very next day, Manley and his men in the **LEE** took the British sloop **POLLY**.

In the meantime, the New Hampshire men in the **WARREN** captured the British supply vessel **RAINBOW** off Portsmouth. She carried, among other foodstuffs for the British Army, 550 bushels of potatoes from Halifax. The **WARREN** also captured the 70-ton **SALLY**, out of Bermuda filled with wine and manned by British tars from the **H.M.S. NIGER**. Two additions to Washington's fleet were the 14-gun schooner **HARRISON** which Ben Tupper captured with his whaleboats off Martha's Vineyard, and the brigantine **WASHINGTON**, outfitted as battle cruisers at Plymouth, Massachusetts in early November. The former was commanded by William Coit and manned by 50 Connecticut men, and the 14-gun **WASHINGTON** sailed with 74 Rhode Island Militiamen under the command of Sion Martindale.

Out only two days, the **HARRISON** captured two Nova Scotian merchantmen off Cape Cod. Captain Coit brought them into Plymouth and landed his prisoners at Plymouth Rock. The **WASHINGTON** took as a prize the Nova Scotian sloop **BRITANNIA** on November 27, on her way to deliver supplies to the British troops. From Boston, General Howe wrote to the Earl of Dartmouth in England on December 13, that, *"rebel privateers are infesting the bay, who can take advantage of many inlets on the coast, where His Majesty's ships cannot pursue them."* General Howe then proposed that, *"provisions and other valuable stores be sent out in the future in ships-of-war, or in vessels of sufficient force to defend themselves against these pirates."*

Despite the presence of British warships, Washington's fleet successfully captured the armed British schooner **FISHER** on December 6th, the British sloop **BETSEY** on December 17th, and on December 9th, the **LEE** brought into Beverly and Salem, the 300-ton cargo-ship **JENNY** and the 150-ton brigantine **LITTLE HANNAH**. The **BETSEY** not only carried needed food but also important British documents on troop movements, which Washington called, *"little inferior to any prize our famous Captain Manley has taken."* The **JENNY** carried a cargo of *"porter, coal, cannons, blunder-buses, and 40 live pigs."* The cargo of the **LITTLE HANNAH**, was *"130 puncheons of rum, 100 cases of gin, limes and oranges,"* as Moylan said, *"to please the delicate appetite of Lord Howe"* — but it was Washington's Navy in Beverly and his Army in Cambridge that consumed the cargo. Also aboard the **LITTLE HANNAH** was a quantity of cinchons, a herb used as a medicine to cure many ills, which Washington said, *"is more precious than tons of gold dust."*

Although pleased with his hero, *"our famous Captain Manley,"* Washington had other words for the commanders and crews of the **WASHINGTON** and **HARRISON**. *"They are wild and unruly and deserted their ships,"* he wrote. Moylan said that, *"the General is much surprised, for the crews are stripping the prizes of every little thing they can lay their hands upon."* The **HARRISON** captured the tiny 15-ton fishing schooner **THOMAS**, carrying a cargo of wine, on December 1st, but Washington declared her *"an improper prize"* and demanded of Captain Coit that he return the schooner and the wine to the rightful owner. On hearing this, the **HARRISON** crew mutinied. Three days later British captain George Montago of the **H.M.S. FOWEY** caught the Rhode Islanders aboard the **WASHINGTON** off guard as they sailed in Boston Bay. The **WASHINGTON** was the first American armed vessel captured by a British man-of-war, and her captain and crew were shipped off to England in chains. Although other captured American and British prisoners were constantly being exchanged during the war, British General Howe refused to exchange the crew of the **WASHINGTON**. Of all the rebel Americans, General Howe hated those of Washington's Navy the most.

Although Congress alloted wages to the crewmen of Washington's fleet in early December, the prize money for enemy ships and cargoes they brought into port was slow in coming. *"The crews are dissatisfied that they cannot get their prize money,"* Washington informed Congress. *"This procrastination is attended with very bad consequences."* By December 31st, the seven month enlistment for most of the crewmen was up, and they left their vessels to return home, angry at not having been paid prize money as promised. *"I am just informed,"* Stephen Moylan wrote to General Reed on January 2, 1776, *"that all the vessels are now in port, the officers and men quitted them; what a pity, as vessels are every day arriving: Indeed, the chance of taking any is pretty well over, as a man-of-war is stationed so as to command the entrance of Beverly, Salem and Marblehead — We must have ships to cope with them."* Undaunted, Washington was determined to revive and reorganize his Navy, for his Army now relied on food, weapons, ammunition and other supplies taken from enemy cargo ships. His first move of the new year was to promote John Manley as Commodore of the fleet and in command of the **HANCOCK**. His other commanders to serve under Manley were new men; Daniel Waters to command the **LEE**, William Burke, the **WARREN**, Samuel Tucker in charge of the **FRANKLIN**, and Charles Dyar, the **HARRISON**.

Washington wanted a sixth vessel to replace his captured namesake, but good sailing ships were in short supply. Most merchants had converted their ships into privateers, hoping to gain financially from the war. New England sailors preferred crewing for privateersmen than joining Washington's Navy, for Congress only allowed one-third of the value of a captured vessel and cargo to be divided among the captain and crew, whereas privateering merchants offered one-half the value of a captured prize to captain and crew. Colonel Lee of Marblehead owned an old idle schooner that was *"iced-in"* across the bay at Manchester Harbor. If Washington's men could chop her out of the ice, Lee would allow Congress to lease it. It took eight men two days to free the schooner **LYNCH** from the harbor ice, and twelve men 18 days to repair the ice damage and refit her at Beverly as a battle cruiser with two cannons and four swivel guns. Washington chose John Ayers to command her.

In early January, sailing in consort, the **LEE and FRANKLIN** converged on the 300-ton brigantine **HENRY AND ESTER**, sailing from Halifax with food and supplies for the British. Approaching the large vessel from both sides, the commanders demanded her surrender and her captain complied without resistance. A week later the same two battle cruisers took another large brig coming into Boston from Nova Scotia, carrying a supply of new British uniforms. The uniforms were stripped of all British insignias and distributed to Washington's rag-tag army troops. The **HANCOCK**, under Captain Manley, started the New Year by seizing two prizes off the coast of Plymouth. Manley also managed to get into a hot cannon duel with the 10-gun battle cruiser **GENERAL GAGE** off Cape Cod, and although the British cruiser was damaged in the exchange of broadsides, she managed to avoid capture by outsailing the **HANCOCK**.

The **HANCOCK** met up with the armed British brig **HOPE** off the coast of Scituate, south of Boston, on January 30, 1776. Under heavy and constant fire from the brig, Manley was forced to run his vessel into the shallows. The larger **HOPE** followed in as close as she could get and continued firing her cannons for five hours. The **HANCOCK** was hit and as she started to sink, Manley and his men abandoned ship and rowed to shore in the **HANCOCK** tenders. Extremely pleased with himself at sinking one of Washington's schooners, Lieutenant George Dawson, commander of the **HOPE**, returned to Boston and informed Vice-Admiral Graves that, *"the HANCOCK is destroyed and many of her men killed."* None of Manley's men were killed, and only three were slightly wounded. Once the **HOPE** had left the scene, the crewmen rowed back out to where the **HANCOCK** sank in the shallows and raised her. She was brought into Scituate and repaired. Two weeks later, with the help of Captain Tucker and his crew in the **FRANKLIN**, the **HANCOCK** captured the 300-ton British transport **SUSANNA** and brought her into Portsmouth. The **SUSANNA** carried food, medicine, cannons and powder.

The **FRANKLIN, HANCOCK, LEE** and **LYNCH** in an all-out *"blitz"*, surprised the 300-ton armed supply ship **STAKESBY**, Boston-bound from London, England. Surrounded by two-thirds of Washington's fleet, the British commander had no choice but surrender or have his vessel blown out of the water. She was escorted into Gloucester and found to carry; *"coal, cheese, live hogs, 180 casks of porter and 50 casks of sourcrout."* With the cheese, pork, porter and sourcrout warming the bellies of Washington's Army on March 17th, seven days after the **STAKESBY** was captured, the British were forced to evacuate Boston, Washington's little Navy having more than a little to do with their hasty departure. The British warships, however, remained off Nantasket Road just outside Boston Harbor for three more months. Although the many British vessels leaving Boston for Halifax, carrying soldiers, Tory families, possessions and other valuables, were escorted by armed men-of-war, they were tantalizing prey for Commodore Manley and his men. On March 21st, the **FRANKLIN, LEE,** and **HANCOCK** managed to overtake one of these transports leaving Boston, loaded with Tories and their riches, but British men-of-war chased off the American cruisers. Two weeks later, the same three schooners chased down the **ELIZABETH**, the last British vessel to leave Boston Harbor, and confiscated all the valuables of the Canadian-bound Tories that were aboard.

With American troops firmly entrenched in Boston, Colonel Artemas Ward took command of Washington's little Navy. The first disappointment for Ward was that Commodore John Manley resigned. His men were disgruntled, angry over the same old subject of not receiving prize money, delayed because of the inefficiency of the Admiralty Courts, and Manley himself wanted to command a larger vessel than the **HANCOCK**. But even with John Manley gone and the pay still slow in coming, Washington's fleet survived. Sam Tucker, former commander of the **FRANKLIN**, took over the **HANCOCK**, and another Marbleheader just released from a British prisoner-of-war camp, James Mugford, was named commander of the **FRANKLIN**. When Washington heard that Ward had appointed Mugford as commander of the 4-gun **FRANKLIN**, he was upset and immediately sent off a dispatch to Ward, telling him not to appoint Mugford, who Washington called a man *"of defamatory character."* The dispatch came too late, for Mugford and his crew of 20 had sailed for Nantasket Road where, Mugford had heard in prison, a large convoy of ships filled with munitions and gunpowder from England was soon to rendezvous with the British fleet.

When a convoy of 12 British transports arrived off Boston, on May 17th, Vice-Admiral Graves' fleet was there to greet them and redirect them to Halifax, but Mugford in the little **FRANKLIN** was there too. He approached the first and largest vessel in the convoy, the 300-ton **HOPE**, carrying as a defense, six carriage guns and 15 swivel guns. *"Surrender,"* Mugford shouted up to the commander, *"or I will kill your captain and all aboard!"* Mugford and his men boarded the **HOPE**, as the British commander ordered his men to cut the vessel's sails to disable the ship, but the British crew refused to obey orders and surrendered. Mugford then raced to bring the **HOPE** and **FRANKLIN** into Boston Harbor before the British could catch him. He chose a narrow channel,

Pulling Point Gut, to sail the **HOPE** in, thinking it was too shallow for pursuing men-of-war, but the **HOPE** went aground. The **FRANKLIN** continued into port to get help, and soon Glover and 150 Marblehead soldiers were on the scene and managed to free the **HOPE**. Her cargo was; *"2,700 barrels of powder, 1,000 carbines, cannon carriages, artillery and carpenter tools."* *"Of immense worth,"* said Colonel Ward. *"If the prize ship had been filled with gold and diamonds, it would not have caused equal joy nor been of equal value."* When Ward told Washington of the capture, George laughed, probably at himself for having initially opposed the courageous Commander Mugford.

After bringing in the **HOPE**, Mugford and his men immediately turned the **FRANKLIN** around and sailed back out Boston Harbor in hopes of catching another valuable supply ship. Heading out with him was the little Boston privateer **LADY WASHINGTON** with six men, under Captain John Frazer. Ironically, sailing out of Pulling Point Gut, the **FRANKLIN** struck a bar and grounded. The **LADY WASHINGTON** sailed in and anchored nearby. Within the hour, 13 whaleboats armed with swivel-guns and carrying a total of 200 men, came cruising down the gut. They were British, from the men-of-war anchored off Nantasket, intent on capturing the **FRANKLIN**. Mugford gave them a broadside with two cannons, stuffing musketballs rather than cannonballs in the muzzles. One whaleboat was hit and sunk. The others rowed in as the **FRANKLIN** crew loaded their muskets and readied their hand spears and swords. The **LADY WASHINGTON** fired her cannons and managed to sink another whaleboat, as she too was surrounded by boats carrying British soldiers intent on boarding her. As Redcoats attempted to board the **FRANKLIN**, Captain Mugford was shot in the stomach. He fell to the deck and called for his Lieutenant Russell. *"I am a dead man,"* he said to Russell, *"but don't give up the vessel. You will be able to beat them off."* As Mugford gasped his last breath, the **FRANKLIN** crew went into a frenzy, shooting, stabbing and clubbing every Redcoat who tried to board. The seven men aboard the **LADY WASHINGTON** fought just as furiously, chopping off British hands the moment they grasped the gunwales. The battle lasted for over a half hour and the whaleboats withdrew without accomplishing their mission. The British lost 70 men, but only two Americans were killed, including Captain James Mugford. As Colonel Ward later commented, *"the name of Captian Mugford ought to be immortalized in America."*

Captain John Skimmer replaced Mugford as commander of the **FRANKLIN**, and the fleet commanders, now with new vengeance, chased after the British convoy that Mugford had alerted them was off the coast and heading for Halifax. The **LEE, WARREN** and **LYNCH** caught up with the 10-gun supply ship **ANN**, *"laden with arms and 94 Highlanders aboard."* They brought the **ANN** into Marblehead and the Scots soldiers into Plymouth as prisoners-of-war. On the same day, June 6th, Jeremiah O'Brien in the **MACHIAS LIBERTY**, who had sailed south to join in the fun, captured a sloop and schooner off Cape Ann and sent them into Newburyport. Another of the British convoy, the 240-ton **PEGGY**, carrying eight guns and a cargo of *"foodstuffs, wine and strong beer,"* was *"blitzed"* by Washington's fleet and brought into Marblehead, as were the 220-ton **GEORGE** and the 120-ton brig **ANNA BELLE**, after a four hour battle at sea. After this hard-fought battle, Captain Tucker of the **HANCOCK** complained that his pine tree flag was *"riddled to pieces,"* and therefore he couldn't have struck it if he had been forced to. The **GEORGE** and **ANNA BELLE** struck their flags finally, with four men killed and ten wounded aboard the British vessels, and only four American seamen slightly wounded. On June 19th, Washington's entire fleet, excepting the **LYNCH**, overpowered the 200-ton British brig **LORD HOWE**, crowded with British soldiers, mainly Highlanders, and with them, their Battalion Commander, Colonel Lawrence Campbell. That same day, Captain Burke in the **WARREN**, captured another 300-ton member of the British convoy, but one of his own cannons blew up, killing three of the **WARREN** crew and wounding seven. He was forced to return to port without his prize ship. A month later, with the **LYNCH**, the **WARREN** attempted to capture the British battle cruiser **H.M.S. LIVERPOOL**, but instead, the **WARREN** was captured and Captain Burke and his crew were shipped off to Halifax as prisoners.

The **LYNCH** lost her commander John Ayers, when he got into a heated arguement with the Boston prize agent and was kicked out of Washington's fleet. The new commander of the **LYNCH**, John Adams, did not join the other commanders of the fleet in capturing British supply ships, but sailed the **LYNCH** in a continuous route from America to France and back, delivering dispatches. The **LYNCH** was finally captured by a man-of-war off Plymouth, England. The **HARRISON**, her commander Charles Dyar and 36 seamen were mustered out of Washington's Navy in March of '76, the Commander-in-Chief not satisfied with the actions of the vessel or her commander. The **HANCOCK, FRANKLIN** and **LEE** continued in service, capturing many more British prizes, until December of 1776, when the **HANCOCK** and **FRANKLIN** were returned to their owners at Marblehead and her crewmen returned to service in John Glover's regiment. It was these crewmen who rowed Washington's Army across the ice-choked Delaware River in whaleboats for the important victory at Trenton. The **LEE**, the last of Washington's fleet, wasn't decommissioned until October 26, 1777, and alone, under command of John Skimmer who replaced Captain Waters, she captured nine more British prizes within nine months. The most successful of Washington's little Navy was the **HANCOCK**. She captured a total of 40 enemy vessels. Although the fleet had its ups and downs and sometimes caused Washington deep regret and embarrasment, these little fighting ships were of great importance in bringing needed supplies to the American Army. With all her growing pains, Washington's little Navy was the acorn from which the mighty oak of the American Navy grew, soon spreading sails upon the waters of the world.

Two commanders in George Washington's Navy, Nicholson Broughton (left) and James Mugford, both from Marblehead, Massachusetts. Washington didn't like either one of them, but the General changed his mind when Mugford became a martyred hero. The schooner HANNAH, commanded by Broughton, sailed out of Beverly, Massachusetts, and is considered "the first ship of the American Navy." - Drawing by Paul Hawthorne. Photos of portraits and drawing, courtesy of the Peabody Museum, Salem, MA. The barracks for Washington's Navy and local privateersmen, is still standing and presently being restored by the Beverly Historical Society, on Water Street, Beverly, MA.

III
SHAPE UP AND SHIP OUT

When war erupted with the greatest maritime nation in the world, America was unprepared in every way. George Washington's whaleboats and little schooners, although surprisingly successful, were no match for the British Navy. Prior to the Revolution, because of intense lobbying of Parliament by English merchants, Americans were resticted from building merchant vessels for themselves, yet one-third of all British vessels plying the high seas in 1774 had been built in America. New England-built ships were faster and more sturdy than those built in England and cheaper to construct here, where durable oak for the hulls and flexible pine for the masts were readily available in our vast forests. Yankee ship builders and sail makers were also constantly experimenting with new hull and sail designs in an attempt to make swifter vessels manned by fewer crew members with greater cargo space. It was Andrew Robinson of Gloucester, Massachusetts who converted a sloop into a larger vessel that could hold double the cargo, need only half the crew that the sloop required, and sail faster with two masts and no added canvas. By so doing, he invented the most popular vessel of the 18th century — the schooner.

America produced more iron for cannons, cannon-balls, and shipboard fittings than England, but Parliament had managed to strictly regulate the construction of cannons in New England. The *"Iron Act"* of 1750 forbade the production of cannons and cannon-balls in America, for it competed with the munitions industry in England. Yet in the early 1700s, cannons were so prevalent in New England that instead of signposts, cannons marked the corners of main streets in the port towns. Because of the desperate need for ship cannons in America when the Revolution began, these old street markers were dug up and used by Yankee privateersmen.

"Even the tall masts that bears your flag," an embittered Boston sea captain told Vice-Admiral Graves, *"grew in our soil and ripened in our sky."* He was referring to the majestic pine forests of Maine that were set aside for exclusive use by the King's Navy in 1691. For over eighty years, many of the tall pine trees of the Maine woods were periodically marked with the symbol of a broad arrow by the agents of the Crown, destined to be cut down and shipped to England for the masts of Royal Naval vessels. If any Yankee dare cut one down or even attempt to build a home near a pine marked with a broad arrow, he would be whipped and shipped off to England for years of imprisonment. In

1775, however, when the New England craze for privateering began, the King's marked pines were the first to go. There was hardly a seaside or riverside village or town from the New York border to Machiasport that didn't boast of at least one shipyard, and the fastest growing industry in New England in 1775-76, was ship-building. All the local businessmen wanted ships as fast as the yards could build them, but their stimulus wasn't all patriotic fervor — it was also greed.

By the spring of 1775, New England commerce was in near-ruin, with all major ports either occupied or blockaded by the British. Over 30,000 American seamen and fishermen, mostly New Englanders, were out of work. Then, when most Americans felt that reconciliation with Britain was still possible and desirable, the King himself decided to stop all merchant trade to America, hoping to *"starve the Rebels into submission."* Most New England vessels were needed for off-shore fishing in order to feed the populace, and fishermen were exempt from military duty, but boat owners and fishermen were enticed away from the fishing grounds by the lure of privateering. The old Yankee smugglers, their backs to the wall once again, quickly prepared their merchant vessels for all out war — and profit. As Connecticut's Silas Deane so adequately put it to members of the Provincial Congress, *"Seamen, ship owners, and the various mechanics, thrown out of employ in the Northern Colonies, cannot possibly long rest easy in their present destitute, distressed situation, their ships rotting and their families starving. . . . they will pursue the only method in their power for indemnifying themselves. . . ."* This *"only method"* quickly developed into what historian Thomas Clark called, *Privateering fever."* Massachusetts and Rhode Island were first to issue *"letters-of-marque and reprisal,"* allowing local merchants and seamen to go out privateering. The Provincial Congress, still hoping that problems with England would be resolved without war, in June of 1775, notified the thirteen colonies that, *"at your own expense, make such provisions by armed vessels for the protection of your harbors and navigation. . ."* Congress was therefore reluctantly condoning privateering against the British, realizing that this *"left-handed piracy"* would flourish whether they approved of it or not.

Fishermen, farmers, old men and boys, deserters from Washington's Army, and foreign seamen, were coerced and convinced that privateering was adventurous and profitable. There was usually no strict discipline aboard these privately owned ships, rum was always available, and they could take a poke at their snobbish English cousins, or in the case of the French, Spanish, Irish, and Scots seamen recruited, they could take a deserved swipe at an old enemy — and most enticing was that the captain and crew would share one-half of the value of all ships and cargoes captured, enough to possibly make them millionaires. Over 3,000 crewmen were needed out of the port of Salem alone, to man 158 privateers. This was an incredible demand, considering that only 8,000 people lived in that port town at the time. Salem merchants and sea captains went so far as to recruit British tars directly off the English warships that blockaded the harbors along the North Shore of Boston. Recruitment posters delivered directly to British sailors and marines offshore by little boys in rowboats read: *"Your situation is very unhappy under the command of the most vile and miserable wretches that ever disgraced the name of Brit. Gentlemen, the Americans will entertain a respect for you, consider you as brethren, and to live in harmony with you and to make you free citizens of America. May you soon be freed from the service of tyrants. Become the glorious defenders of freedom, and join the victorious Americans."* Surprisingly, many *"Brits"* took up the offer and jumped ship, escaping the harsh discipline and low pay aboard British Navy war cruisers and men-of-war. *"All means were resorted to, which ingenuity could devise, to induce men to enlist,"* said 14 year old Ebenezer Fox of Roxbury, who was himself induced to join the crew of the privateer **PROTECTOR** out of Boston. Although Fox seems too young to be sailing off to war, Revolutionary War records reveal that one out of every twelve crewmen serving aboard American privateers was 15 years old or younger. There were also a few privateers captained by teenagers, and one fighting ship out of Salem had a captain and a ten-man crew, all under the age of twenty-one.

"A recruiting officer, bearing a flag and attended by a band of martial music, paraded the streets to excite the thirst for glory and a spirit of military ambition," wrote Ebenezer Fox. *"My excitable feelings were aroused; I repaired to the rendezvous, signed the ship's papers, mounted a cockade, and in my own estimation, I was already more than half a sailor..."* As the day wore on however, and the new recruits were ordered to board the 20-gun **PROTECTOR** for a six-month cruise against the British, his *"thirst for glory"* wavered: *"Upward to 130 men were carried, dragged and driven on board, of all kinds, ages and descriptions, in all the various stages of intoxication; from that of sober tipsiness to beastly drunkenness, with the uproar and clamor that may be more easily imagined than described. The wind being fair, we weighed anchor..."*

Posters, billboards, flyers, and newspaper advertising were used to fill the needed complement of men and boys so that privateers could get to sea as soon as possible. *"All gentlemen, officers and seamen, that intend to make their Fortune under my command,"* read a large ad in the *Boston Morning Chronicle,* "*are requested to repair on board the* **GENERAL MIFFLIN** — *20-guns, by the 25th of March, where good encouragement will be given* — *signed, George Babcock, Commander.*" Babcock's *"good encouragement"* could mean an advance in pay, credited against shares in the anticipated capture of British goods, or it could mean a bottle of rum. Anything and everything was used to get men to sign on. Simeon Perkins reveals in his diary that farmer Peter Leonard *"will sail aboard the privateer* **LUCY** *as a seaman for one barrel of flower, four gallons of molasses, fourteen pounds of sugar and two shirts."* Most recruits wanted an advance in money or goods against their share in looted enemy ships, to leave something behind for their half-starved families, but some wanted nothing in advance, just the opportunity to battle the British. Stephen Phillips and a friend from Marblehead, after seeing a recruiting poster for privateersmen, walked fifty miles to Portsmouth, New Hampshire to join up. They were deeply disappointed when the commander of the **RANGER** refused to take them aboard as crewmen. The reason the Commander John Paul Jones rejected them was that Stephen and his friend were only twelve years old. After his long walk back home however, Stephen stopped off at Salem where he was allowed to join a privateering crew — he later went on to own his own fleet of Salem merchantmen, and became one of America's first millionaires.

Another youngster beckoned to Salem, to the sea, and the glories of battle by a recruitment poster, was 18 year old farm-hand Joe Peabody of Middleton, Massachusetts. He volunteered as a seamen aboard the privateer **BUNKER HILL**, but out to sea only a few weeks, he fell desperately ill and was returned home. His high fever and accompanying hallucinations lasted for over two months. *"He imagined he was a wealthy Salem merchant,"* his son George Peabody later revealed in a journal, *"but one day, walking in an open field, congratulating himself on his great success, he stopped for a moment to look around, when all his dreams of wealth and distinction vanished in an instant."* The fever broken and his hallucinating over, Joe returned to Salem and signed on as a crewman aboard the privateer **PILGRIM**. The **PILGRIM**, under the command of Hugh Hill, engaged in many battles and had many successes, sending eleven prize British ships into the port of Beverly. One of them was the British brig **SUCCESS**, which had little success when she met up with the **PILGRIM**, and Hill chose Joe Peabody to sail her into Beverly as the prize-master. Joe then sailed in the privateer **RAMBLER** out of Beverly, and on his fifth privateering cruise, was made master of the Salem privateer **FISH HAWK**. The **FISH HAWK** was captured by the British in September of 1781, and Joe Peabody and his crew were locked up in a Newfoundland prison. *"It was a perfect Bedlam,"* Joe later reported, but while in jail another inmate tutored him in arithmetic. In an exchange of prisoners between the British and Americans, Joe was released and he returned to Salem to join yet another privateer, the brig **RANGER**. The **RANGER** headed south to pick up a cargo of flour from George Washington's Mount Vernon plantation to deliver to Havana, Cuba. While anchored in the Potomac River, the **RANGER** was attacked, but not by the British — by pirates, some 200 of them in two boats. As the pirates attempted to board, the commander of the **RANGER**, Thomas Simmons, was shot in the leg and four members of his 20-man crew were wounded. First mate Joe Peabody led the charge in driving off the pirates, but during the battle, a musket ball tore through his wrist and another creased his scalp, removing most of his hair. Joe survived and managed to capture the pirate brig. Three days later, a British man-of-war bombarded the **RANGER** and then chased her up the Atlantic coast for three days. The **RANGER** returned to Salem, and that concluded Joe Peabody's war time experiences, but not his life on the sea. With the money he earned from privateering, he bought a 132-ton brig called **THREE FRIENDS**, and like Stephen Phillips, soon owned a fleet of merchantmen, at one time numbering over 40 vessels— his strange hallucinations during his prolonged illness as a teenager became a reality.

    The man who sent more privateers to sea and profited most from privateering never saw battle, never went to sea himself, and couldn't swim, but he went on to become America's first millionaire. He was the older brother of John Derby, who sailed the **QUERO** to England to let the British know that their battle with America had started. Elias Hasket Derby, *"the tyrant of his day,"* one of his compatriots called him, made it his responsibility to keep the Salem privateers active during the Revolution. The Derbys owned many of Salem's battle-cruisers, and their quarter-mile long wharf extending into the harbor stands today as a national landmark on Derby Street, facing the custom-house and the Derby home. During the war, Elias was most noted for designing and building the famous white-hulled privateer **GRAND TURK**, completed in June of 1781. She had a spoon-shaped bow, an extended bowsprit, two square sails and three small jib-sails, all Derby inventions, which made her one of the swiftest vessels in the privateering fleet. With *"a great spread of canvas,"* she headed for the south coast of Ireland carrying 28-guns and a crew of 120 men and boys under command of Captain Thomas Simmons. After two successful voyages, capturing

British merchant vessels sailing the shipping lanes from Ireland to Liverpool, the captain and every seaman aboard the **GRAND TURK** had enough money from British booty to retire for life. Her second voyage under Captain Joseph Pratt also brought Elias Derby enough money to pay for the building of the ship. Within 22 months of privateering, the **GRAND TURK** took 16 British prizes and delivered them all safely to Elias in Salem.

Not all ship owners who built privateers or converted their merchant vessels into privateers became wealthy. Some went bankrupt. The Cabot family of Beverly who owned many privateers, lost a fortune during the first year of the war, but made up their losses and prospered as the Revolution progressed. John and Patrick Tracy of Newburyport, Massachusetts, not only lost money during the first two years of the war, but lost 41 privateers, either captured by the British or destroyed in battle. One Newburyport privateer, the **NEPTUNE**, capsized leaving port on her maiden voyage and sank. Another Newburyport privateer, **YANKEE HERO**, was captured with her commander Captain James Tracy and 170 crewmen by the **H. M. S. LIVELY**. News of her demise brought mourning throughout the town of Newburyport. By 1779 however, the Tracy brothers had recuperated their losses, their privateers bringing 120 enemy prizes into port, with cargoes valued at $3,950,000. The Tracys donated $167,000 of their profits to George Washington's army. Even Elias Derby lost money during the first year of the Revolution, and 54 privateers from Salem were captured by the enemy during the war.

Life aboard the privateers wasn't always the enjoyable adventure the recruiters promised either. One privateersman aboard the brig **RESOLUTION** lamented that, *"the biscuits are so hard that we often use cannon balls to break them into pieces, and there are so many worms that we just eat them too. The salt-beef is hardened to the consistency of leather, sometimes used to carve scrimshaw. The water we drink is bad, with thick finger-long fibers in it, giving it a glutinous consistency. There is scurvy on board, which loosins the teeth and swells the limbs, with a pain that will kill you..."*

Young Eb Fox also gives us an insight into his first battle experience aboard the 20-gun Massachusetts privateer **PROTECTOR**: *"June 9th— As the fog cleared, we perceived a large ship under English colors fitted out with thirty-two guns, and furnished with a complement of one hundred and fifty men. She was called the ADMIRAL DUFF... The shrill pipe of the boatswain summoned all hands to their duty... The enemy approached till within musket shot of us. I* *particularly noticed the British captain, a noble looking man, having a large gold-laced cocked hat on his head, and a speaking trumpet in his hand. The English captain asked the name of our ship. Lt. Little, in order to gain time, put the trumpet to his ear, pretending not to hear the question. During the short interval thus gained, our Captain Williams called upon the gunner to ascertain how many guns could be brought to bear upon the enemy. 'Five,' was the answer. 'Then fire,' were the orders... The cannons poured forth their deadly contents and the enemy returned the compliment. Broadsides were exchanged with great rapidity for nearly an hour; our fire, as we afterwards ascertained, produced a terrible slaughter among the enemy, while our loss was as yet trifling. A shot from one of our marines killed a man at the wheel of the enemy's ship, and his place not being immediately supplied, she was brought alongside of us in such a manner as to bring her bowsprit directly across our forecastle. Broadside for broadside continued with unabated vigor, at times so near to each other that the muzzles of our guns came almost in contact. The contest was obstinately continued by the enemy, although we could perceive that great havock was made among them. The action had now lasted about an hour and a half, and the fire from the enemy began to slacken, when suddenly we discovered that all the sails on her mainmast were enveloped in a blaze. The fire spread with rapidity, and running down the after-rigging, it soon communicated with her magazine, when her whole stern was blown off. All feelings of hostility now ceased, and those of pity were excited in our breasts for the miserable crew that survived the catastrophe."* So ended 14 year old Eb Fox's baptism under fire, but he went on to experience four more battles, being wounded once.

Joshua Barney, another teenage rebel privateersman, was captain of a merchant vessel by age 15. He was 16 when the Revolutionary War began and he became master's-mate aboard the naval warship **HORNET**, involved in the successful attack by the American fleet on the British at Nassua, Bahamas. He then volunteered as mate aboard the naval ships **WASP, ANDREW DORIA, SARATOGA** and **VIRGINIA**, and was offered a position as first lieutenant aboard the privateer **GENERAL MERCER**. On her first cruise the **MERCER** was chased by a British ship three times her size. As the enemy approached from the stern, British marines were ready to board when Barney cut a hole in the **MERCER**'s stern, slipped a cannon through, loaded it with shot and crowbars, and blew the boarding party and part of the enemy ship away, thus allowing the **MERCER** to make good her escape.

During the Revolution, Barney participated in 36 sea battles, was captured by the British and imprisoned three times, and escaped three times. On his third escape from an English prison, he dressed as a British naval officer and arrived in France as a passenger aboard a Royal coach. Returning to Beverly, Massachusetts, he was offered command of a 20-gun privateer by the Cabot family, but he opted to command the 16-gun **HYDER ALI** that was to lead a convoy of American merchantmen into southern waters. Off Cape May the convoy encountered three British warships, one being the former privateer **FAIR AMERICAN** that had earlier been captured by the British, but for some unknown reason, the Brits hadn't changed her name. The second was the **QUEBEC**, and the third was the 20-gun **GENERAL MONK**, formerly the **GENERAL WASHINGTON**, once commanded by Rhode Island's famous privateersman Silas Talbot, which earlier had been captured by two men-of-war and converted into a British warship. Barney signaled the convoy to move on, as he maneuvered the **HYDER ALI** to face the oncoming warships.

The **FAIR AMERICAN** got off one volley of cannon balls, missed Barney's privateer, then accidentally grounded on a sandbar. The **QUEBEC** was too far off to do Barney's ship any damage, but the **GENERAL MONK** closed in, hoping to have her marines board the smaller **HYDER ALI**. Included in the 120-man crew of the **HYDER ALI** was a complement of sharpshooting back-woodsmen, who Barney had wisely invited to join him on his cruise. When the **GENERAL MONK** came alongside, Barney barked out orders to his helmsman, loud enough for the commander of the British ship to hear. *"Hard to port,"* he shouted, but earlier he had told the helmsman to sail in exactly the opposite direction of his commands, so the **HYDER ALI** swung to starboard instead of port, catching the British off-guard. Barney's starboard cannons raked the deck of the **GENERAL MONK** as the two ships side-swiped each other, and the back-woodsmen in the rigging of the **HYDER ALI** started hitting the British naval officers and marines one by one with their long rifles. The British surrendered within a half-hour.

Barney was then made commander of his prize, changing her name back to the original **GENERAL WASHINGTON**. Sailing her into her old home port of Providence, Rhode Island, Barney was given a heroes welcome at Newport, including a ten-gun salute from shore. In Narragansett Bay, Barney decided to return the salute from his ship, but he forgot that his deck cannons were still loaded with cannonballs. The cheering crowd on shore quickly dispersed in horror as cannonballs rained down on them. No one was killed, but two buildings were destroyed and one spectator lost his foot in Barney's surprising but accidental broadside. The street called *"Barney's Alley"* in Newport, where one of his cannonballs landed, is named for this daring teenaged privateersman.

   Like Barney's **HYDER ALI**, merchants and privateersmen often gave unusual names to their fighting vessels. Hyder Ali was an Indian prince who was very anti-British, and Barney's ship was named for him. One Rhode Island privateer was named **YE TERRIBLE CREATURE**, and another was given the name **THINKS I TO MYSELF THINKS I**, obviously owned by merchants with Irish roots. Scotsman John Paul Jones' famous flagship **BONHOMME RICHARD**, or *"Goodman Richard,"* was named for Ben Franklin's wise old friend Richard Saunders, who was immortalized in Franklin's *"Poor Richard's Almanac."* John Paul Jones also commanded the **RANGER**, named for Timothy Murphy, one of Daniel Morgan's Rangers, whose sharpshooting turned the tide of battle into an American victory at Saratoga. There were at least four other privateers; a brig, schooner, sloop, and ketch called **RANGER** during the Revolution. Jones also commanded the naval 12-gun sloop **PROVIDENCE**, and there were at least three vessels called **PROVIDENCE** during the war; the aforementioned sloop, a 28-gun frigate, both built at Providence, Rhode Island, and a three-gun gondola, one of General Arnold's fleet battling the British on Lake Champlain. Benedict Arnold's flagship on the lake was the 10-gun galley **WASHINGTON**, which could be rowed or sailed. She was badly damaged and captured by the British in the Battle of Valcour Island. Strangely, as in the case of the privateer **FAIR AMERICAN**, the British adopted the **WASHINGTON** into their lake navy, but didn't change her name. There were probably twenty vessels of various sizes and descriptions named **WASHINGTON**, **GENERAL WASHINGTON** and **LADY WASHINGTON** active during the war.

   There were many Revolutionary War vessels with the name **AMERICA** or **AMERICAN** in them. General Arnold's 10-gun gondola **AMERICAN CONVERT** was also captured by the British, and renamed **LOYAL CONVERT**. Maine's privateer schooner **AMERICA**, sailing out of Sebascoden Island, captured the British privateer **PICAROON** and brought her into the Harpswell Islands, where most of her British captives eventually became American citizens. The battleship **AMERICA**, the Continental Navy's only vessel touting 74 cannons, was built in Portsmouth, New Hampshire, and was to be commanded by John Paul Jones. Because the French man-of-war

MAGNIFIQUE, also to be commanded by Jones, sank accidentally in Boston Harbor, Congress gave the **AMERICA** to the French, and Jones, losing command of both ships, was furious. There was the **YANKEE AMERICAN** out of Salem, the **YANKEE** out of Bristol, Rhode Island, the **TRUE BLOODED YANKEE** out of Boston, the **YANKEE PORTER** out of Connecticut, the **YANKEE HERO** out of Newburyport, and the **YANKEE RANGER** of Providence, Rhode Island, plus many more privateers that included the name *"Yankee"* painted on the stern.

The name **DOLPHIN**, for some unknown reason, also seemed to be a popular name for privateers. The navy had a 14-gun privateer cutter named **DOLPHIN**, under command of Sam Nicholson, noted for capturing twenty British merchant ships off the coasts of England and France. Even Ben Franklin sponsored a privateer **DOLPHIN**, in hopes of capturing British sailors that he could use in exchange for Americans suffering in British prison ships and jails. Another **DOLPHIN**, under command of Nat Hayward, was unique in that it could fit ten sails on one mast and could outdistance any pursuing British frigate. Another privateer **DOLPHIN** of Salem, it was said, *"would often leave port in the morning and return before night with a prize."* Her mate was a giant of a man named Hodges who had six brothers, all serving on privateers out of Salem and Beverly. One brother was captured when the privateer he served on was taken by the **H.M.S. LIVELY**. The British commander couldn't believe the height of young Ben Hodges — he was six feet, six inches tall, an enormous size in the 1700s, when the average man's height was 5'5". Hodges informed the surprised commander that *"I am the shortest member of my family."*

The smallest member of America's privateering fleet was the little fishing boat **WASP** out of Marblehead. She carried no cannons, her nine-man crew stinging the British with muskets, clubs, and cutlasses. Another **WASP** was a Continental Navy cruiser of eight guns that was purposely blown up by her crew in the Delaware River to avoid capture by the British. The largest American ship battling the British was the French built 32-gun frigate **DEANE**, carrying a complement of 210 Yankee sailors and marines. After a few small successes, the **DEANE** remained tied to a dock in Boston, her commander unable to recruit the number of men needed to man her sails and guns. Yet, before the war was half over, it was estimated that there were more men crewing in American privateers than there were in George Washington's Army.

The Commonwealth of Massachusetts, including Maine, commissioned over 500 privateers, with a few like the **PROTECTOR** that the governor and legislature sponsored and paid for. Rhode Island issued about 100 letters-of-marquis, and Connecticut, over 50. New Hampshire, operating out of Portsmouth, had some 20 privateers, and the Continental Congress, who didn't issue commissions to privately owned ships until April 3, 1776, recorded a total of 1,700 privateers operating during the Revolutionary War. New England privateers alone captured and sank an estimated 1,450 enemy vessels. The tide of the war began to turn on the high seas in favor of America in 1777, when, in that one year, our privateers took a total of 733 British merchant vessels and warships.

Once the New England privateersmen had shaped up and shipped out, there was no stopping their devastation on the British. Their bold activities off this coast cost Vice-Admiral Graves his job. He was eventually called back to England in disgrace because of his inability to stop *"those pirating rascals from taking British supply ships,"* and his failure to adequately blockade port towns in an effort to *"starve the Rebels into submission."* In the West Indies, where British subjects remained loyal to the Crown, New England privateersmen captured one out of every four enemy vessels trading or cruising in the Caribbean. They were so successful that rum and sugar, two of New Englanders' favorite consumer items, dropped drastically in price at home; 100 pounds of sugar dropping in price to only $5.00 and Jamaica Rum selling for 75 cents a gallon. The privateersmen slowly but surely solved America's food problem, and in England, where merchants were at first annoyed with American privateersmen, and then publicly panic-striken, a heavy blow was felt in their bread-basket. The British ambassador to Spain let his fears be known in a letter to Parliament. It read in part; *"A fleet of our vessels came from Ireland a few days ago. From sixty vessels that departed, not above twenty-eight arrived here, the others, it is thought, being all taken by American privateers... If this American War continues, we shall all die of hunger..."*

Although many New England privateersmen sailed directly from home ports to battle the British in their own backyard off the coast of England, Ben Franklin was instrumental in allowing them to sail out of ports in France and to use them as safe harbors. One of these privateers out of Boston was the **GENERAL MIFFLIN**. Lord Stormont, the British ambassador to France said that this vessel *"committed great depredations along the English Coast."* The ambassador complained that the **GENERAL MIFFLIN** *"is being harbored by the French at the port of Brest,"* and he threatened that England would break off friendly relations with France if the French continued to protect American privateers. *"All American vessels are to leave French ports,"* the French authorities announced publicly, but the Americans didn't heed the order and the French didn't enforce it. France officially joined America as her ally in 1778.

The most active English port of Liverpool was molested by privateersmen beyond endurance, and even though English merchant vessels were often escorted by British warships, the port of Liverpool eventually was forced to close down. English merchants were frightened and furious, for by February 1777, 250 Liverpool vessels had been captured with cargoes valued at over ten-million dollars, off the coasts of England and Ireland. The American privateers often took British ships two to four times their size. Yankee privateersmen were too daring and reckless for the likes of the conservative British merchants, who were losing a fortune. *"The immense naval force of Great Britain was rendered incompetent to fully protect her own shipping,"* wrote historian of the day Thomas Clark. *"They were rendered incompetent by the privateers of a country that possessed not a single sail of the line, and that had been only a year in existence as a nation."*

America's three greatest sea-warriors of the Revolution: Silas Talbot out of Providence, Rhode Island; John Paul Jones out of Portsmouth, New Hampshire; and Jon Haraden out of Salem, Massachusetts. Portraits courtesy of the Rhode Island Historical Society, Providence, and the Essex Institute and Peabody Museum, Salem, MA.

The GRAND TURK, owned by Elias Derby of Salem, was one of the largest, speediest, and most successful privateers of the Revolution. The American Navy frigate HANCOCK, commanded by John Manley, George Washington's favorite skipper, was captured by the British, and considered by them to be "the finest frigate afloat." This painting of the HANCOCK with tattered sails, was by the British artist Francis Holmad in 1779. Photos of paintings courtesy of the Peabody Museum, Salem, MA. Copy of broadside, popular during the Revolution, introducing a new song about Commander John Manley and his many heroic exploits - courtesy Peabody Museum, Salem, MA. America's first Marine, wearing a green and white uniform, black hat, and a leather collar to protect his neck against swords and cutlasses - thus the nick-name "leather-necks." Most of America's first Marines were foreigners. Drawing by Peter F. Copeland, courtesy Dover Publications of New York, from "Uniforms of the American Revolution."

IV
DON'T TREAD ON ME

Although many New England seaside towns seemingly hold legitimate claim to be *"Birthplace of The American Navy,"* it was little Rhode Island that first organized a state navy, and was first to suggest and petition the Provincial Congress to sponsor a national navy. The petition was introduced by two Congressmen, Steve Hopkins and Sam Ward, who had both served as governors of Rhode Island, but in early October 1775, their plea fell on deaf ears. John Adams of Massachusetts and Silas Deane of Connecticut also lobbied their fellow congressmen, but most representatives from the Southern Colonies were opposed to an American Navy. Their reasoning was that it would be too costly. *"It's the maddest idea in the world,"* said Congressman Samuel Chase of Maryland, *"requiring Congress to mortgage the entire continent."*

When Captain John Barry, a native Irishman, arrived at Philadelphia in his merchantman **BLACK PRINCE** in October, he informed Congress that British merchant vessels were about to depart England for Nova Scotia without a naval escort. Silas Deane suggested to Congress that privateers from Rhode Island and Connecticut be hired to intercept these munitions ships, and Congress agreed. One of the vessels hired was the 12-gun Rhode Island sloop **KATY**, under command of Abe Whipple of **GASPEE** fame. As early as June 12, 1775, Rhode Island had armed and manned two privateers to deal with the 24-gun **H.M.S. ROSE**, commanded by the harsh British lieutenant James Wallace, who was capturing merchant vessels and cargoes in Narragansett Bay. Wallace also demanded food and supplies for his crew from the people of Newport, threatening to burn down the town if he didn't get cooperation. *"I will hang Abraham Whipple at the yardarm,"* he announced to the Rhode Islanders, and Whipple replied in a note to the lieutenant, telling him that, *"You always must catch a man before you hang him."* In the **KATY**, Whipple and his crew managed to attack and capture the British naval sloop **DIANA**, the **ROSE**'s tender, on June 15, 1775. It is considered to be *"the first authorized capture of a British naval vessel in the Revolutionary War."* When Congress hired the **KATY**, she was renamed **PROVIDENCE**, and is hailed by Rhode Islanders as *"the first ship of the American Navy."* Getting Congress to hire merchant vessels and privateers was considered a great breakthrough by Silas Deane, and he wrote to his friend Tom Mumford, *"... and I have prospect of carrying that point, having succeeded in getting our Connecticut and Rhode Island vessels into Continental pay... I am of your opinion that New London Harbor is well suited for rendeyvous of an*

American Navy."

Information from George Washington's spies that eight British warships and troopships were heading to Boston, carrying five regiments of Redcoats and 1,000 British Marines, and word that Vice-Admiral Graves intended to bombard many New England port towns, finally convinced Congress that a national navy was needed. A Naval Committee, most of its members New Englanders, was established, and within three months, America's first naval fleet was prepared to sail from Philadelphia to meet the enemy. John Adams wrote the rules and regulations for the new navy and is therefore often referred to as *"The Father of the U.S. Navy."* The Commodore, or Commander-In-Chief of the fleet was Rhode Island's Esek Hopkins, brother of the congressman, and he too is claimant of the title, *"Father of the Navy."* John Barry's merchant vessel **BLACK PRINCE** was given 30 cannons and became the flagship of the fleet — John Barry is also considered *"The Father of the American Navy."* Dudley Saltonstall of New London, Connecticut, Silas Deane's brother-in-law, was chosen as commander of the **BLACK PRINCE**, which was renamed **ALFRED** — often referred to as *"The First Ship of the American Navy." "She was named in honor of the founder of the greatest navy that ever existed,"* said John Adams — King Alfred, founder of the British Navy. The British also had an **ALFRED**, a 76-gun man-of-war, patrolling America's East Coast.

Other members of what was called then, *"The American Squadron,"* were; the **COLUMBUS**, 28-guns, 300 men, commander Abe Whipple, the Commodore's nephew, the **CABOT**, 14-guns, 200 seamen, under command of John Hopkins, the Commodore's son, and the **ANDREW DORIA**, 16-guns, 200 men, commanded by Nicholas Biddle. Nepotism was ripe in America's new navy. The sloop **PROVIDENCE** and the six-gun **FLY** joined the four frigates at anchor in the Deleware River in early January, 1776. The latter two were also commanded by Rhode Island men, John Hazard and Hoystead Hacker. The only commander not from Rhode Island or Connecticut, was Nicholas Biddle from Pennsylvania, and he was the only commander with naval experience. He had been a midshipman in the British Navy, and was only 24 years old. Hazard had brought with him a yellow flag, which he turned over to Esek Hopkins to be flown as the *"flag of the flotilla."* In the middle of the flag was the symbol of a rattlesnake, and below it the words, *"Don't Tread On Me."* The first lieutenant of the flagship **ALFRED** raised the new flag to the masthead, below George Washington's Grand Union flag of 13 red and white stripes, with the Union Jack in the upper corner. This first lieutenant was John Paul Jones,

"Father of the American Navy."

Recruiting enough qualified seamen to serve in the new navy and for the Marines Corps, which was established by Congress on November 9, 1775, was not an easy task. Congress wanted *"good seamen, or those aquainted with maritime affairs,"* to become America's first sailors and marines. They even offered a bounty of eight dollars *"to the public and to the owner of every American vessel, for every able seaman that he shall import into the United Colonies, and that foreigners importing able seamen over and above the ship's company, and discharging them in American ports, shall be intitled to the same bounty."* The incentive to join the navy and see the world, under strict naval discipline, couldn't compete with the free-spirited life on privateers. Although the Naval and Marine Committees of Congress offered *"one-half of the value of all enemy ships of war captured"* to the new naval and marine recruits, only one-third the value of merchant vessels and their cargoes was offered. Foreign seamen, however, liked the deal, and of the first forty men recruited into the American Navy and Marines, 32 were from England, Scotland, Wales, Ireland, Germany, France and Holland — only eight were American born. Most of them were inexperienced in sea battle, as were their commanders. Yet, the enemy they were going out to face were well trained and experienced, sailing in bigger and better armed ships.

With some 1,000 sailors in blue uniforms and 200 marines dressed in green, the six-vessel squadron was ready to depart by mid January. They would meet up with two supporting vessels out of Baltimore at Cape Henlopen, the 10-gun **HORNET** and the 8-gun **WASP**. Commadore Hopkins had orders from Congress to attack former Royal Governor Lord Dunmore's pirating vessels that were patrolling the Virginia coast, then he was to destroy or capture all enemy vessels blockading the Carolinas, and finally, sail to Rhode Island in an attempt to rid that coast of British vessels. Hopkins and his men were eager, but *"The American Squadron"* couldn't move. They were stuck, ice-locked, and they couldn't get out of the Delaware River until February 17, 1776 when the ice melted enough for the ships to slip into the Atlantic. The Commodore, however, decided not to go to Virginia or the Carolinas, but to Nassua in the Bahamas, where he knew the British stored munitions and other supplies desperately needed by George Washington's Army. When the Southern Congressmen heard that the American Navy's first Commander-In-Chief had disobeyed Congressional orders and had bypassed their troubled colonies, the new navy was in deep trouble before it even got its feet wet.

The **PROVIDENCE** was first to drop off her contingent of marines at Nassua on March 3, 1776. The marines easily took Fort Montague and then Fort Nassua, for both were weakly defended, and they captured the Royal Governor of the Bahamas as well. Confiscated in the American Navy's first amphibious raid were: 150 barrels of powder, 40 cannons and 15 brass mortars. The success of the raid was marred however, for as Commander Biddle relates, *"small-pox broke out aboard and raged with great violence among the seamen, the greater part of whom were New Englanders."* This epidemic forced Hopkins to sail the fleet back up the East Coast toward New London, Connecticut, where he hoped to hospitalize his sick men.

Off the coast of Long Island, on the evening of April 5th, the **ALFRED** and the **CABOT** were attacked by the 20-gun British corvette **GLASCOW**. Early in the battle the **CABOT** was badly damaged by a broadside, with 14 of her seamen killed and seven badly wounded — she retreated. The **ALFRED** battled on for over two hours, losing her tiller, mainbrace, and 13 men killed and wounded in the action. The **GLASCOW** then fixed her guns on the **COLUMBUS** and gave her a devastating broadside, then disappeared into the night, victorious. Congress, especially its Southern members, considered the battle and the clean escape of the **GLASCOW**, *"a disgrace to the American Navy."* To make matters even more humiliating for Commodore Hopkins, was that on the same day of the **GLASCOW** attack, Commander John Barry in the privateer **LEXINGTON** single handedly won a brilliant and hard fought battle over the British sloop **EDWARD**. Hopkins' fleet limped into New London, where his dead, wounded, and 180 sailors and marines suffering from small-pox were put ashore. While in port, Hopkins made another mistake — he gave the cannons and munitions captured at Nassua to the Connecticut and Rhode Island Militia to bolster their defenses, which Congress concluded he had no right to do without congressional approval.

After moving the fleet from New London to Providence, Rhode Island, Hopkins was ordered to come before Congress with his commanders Whipple, Saltonstall and Hazard, *"to answer for their conduct and mal-practices."* At Philadelphia, charges against Whipple and Saltonstall were dropped, but Commander John Hazard was found guilty of *"neglect of duty."* His crew complained that he had whipped them and that he had embezzled naval supplies. John Paul Jones said that Hazard was *"of a rude, unhappy temper,"* and so Hazard was the first naval officer ever drummed out of the military service. Jones replaced him as commander of the **PROVIDENCE**. Commodore Hopkins was censured by Congress, but allowed to continue on as Commodore. John Adams felt that Hopkins was *"unduly persecuted by that anti-New England spirit which haunted Congress."* Although the Commodore did manage to convince Congress that naval crewmen should share in one-half the profits of all merchant prizes taken, he continued to complain that, *"I am at a loss how we shall get the ships manned."* He had even offered new recruits an advance in pay, but almost half of them, once they received their money, deserted the navy and *"went off in privateers."* Hopkins was finally released from his duties as Commodore, and Nicholas Biddle replaced him.

Undaunted by the lack of available manpower, Biddle took the **DORIA** and **CABOT** to sea, and off Rhode Island, captured two British transports with 400 Scots Highlanders aboard them. Biddle bragged that he took them both *"with only my speaking trumpet."* He also convinced many of his Scots prisoners to join the American Navy. Given command of a new naval flagship the 32-gun **RANDOLPH**, he sailed for the West Indies. Off Barbadoes, the **RANDOLPH** met up with the 62-gun man-of-war **YARMOUTH**. They manuevered and dueled for almost an hour, but then the **YARMOUTH** literally blew the **RANDOLPH** out of the water. Commander Biddle was sitting in a chair on deck, tending a wound, when his ship exploded. He, with 314 officers and crew disappeared in a flash. *"Only the American ensign, rolled up, was thrown upon the YARMOUTH forcastle, unsinged,"* a British tar reported, *"and only three Yankee crewmen survived the blast."*

Congress finally relented to Silas Deane's constant plea to build naval ships instead of converting old merchant vessels, and orders for building 13 frigates were passed on to the shipyards in early 1776 — six of them to be built in New England. The 32-gun **HANCOCK** and 24-gun **BOSTON**, at Salisbury and Newburyport, Massachusetts, the 32-gun **WARREN** and a new 28-gun **PROVIDENCE**, at Rhode Island, the 28-gun **TRUMBULL** in Connecticut, and the 32-gun **RALEIGH** at Portsmouth, New Hampshire. Biddle's **RANDOLPH**, built in Philadelphia, was one of these new naval vessels. It took only 60 days to build the frigate **RALEIGH**, and she was launched in May of '76. Her commander was New Hampshire's Thomas Thompson, and he sailed in consort with the **ALFRED**, now under command of Elisha Hinman of Connecticut. Sailing off the West Indies, they were attacked by two lesser British vessels, the 20-gun **ARIADNE** and the 16-gun **CERES**. After a brief exchange of fire *"of only ten minutes,"* reported Thompson, *"Hinman hauled down her colors"* and the **ALFRED**, America's first flagship, surrendered. Thompson, in the 32-gun frigate

RALEIGH, then ran with the two British vessels chasing him for 19 hours. He finally made it safely into Boston, where the recently established national Navy Board called his retreat, *"a disgraceful business."* Thompson was relieved of his command and John Barry took over as commander of the **RALEIGH**.

When the **RALEIGH** weighed anchor under Barry, the British were waiting for her outside Boston Harbor. The 22-gun **UNICORN** and the 50-gun **EXPERIMENT**, commanded by Sir James Wallace, Whipple's old antagonist, chased the **RALEIGH** for almost three days and nights. Off the coast of Penobscot, Barry decided to stop running, and he turned his frigate around to face the **UNICORN** in battle. He hoped he could take or destroy the **UNICORN** before the slower moving **EXPERIMENT** could catch up to them. In his quick turning manuever however, the **RALEIGH**'s foretop mast cracked, rigging and sails falling to the deck and causing confusion. Taking advantage of this mishap, the **UNICORN** sailed in and gave the **RALEIGH** a series of effective broadsides, killing and wounding 32 American sailors and seriously damaging the frigate. The **RALEIGH** returned fire, but with the **EXPERIMENT** closing in, Barry decided to smash the **RALEIGH** on the rocky Maine shore to avoid capture. The British warships followed her in, bombarding her all the way to shore. The crew didn't have time to torch their vessel once she grounded, for a British landing party was quickly aboard, capturing 134 members of the **RALEIGH** crew. Barry and 85 of his crewmembers managed to escape through the woods and up the Penboscot River, slowly making their way back to Boston. The British salvaged and repaired the **RALEIGH**, adopting her into the British Navy without changing her name.

The new frigates **HANCOCK** and **BOSTON** cruised together, although their commanders, John Manley, George Washington's favorite skipper, and Hector McNeill, hated each other. McNeill once told the Navy Board that Manley *"is ignorant, obstinate, overbearing, and tyranical beyond measure."* Together however, they battled and beat the 28-gun frigate **FOX** off the coast of Maine, the fire being so hot at times that both sides twice agreed to interrupt the battle to squelch flames and to cool down their cannons. All three vessels were badly damaged, but heading back to Boston, three British warships, the 44-gun **RAINBOW**, the 32 -gun **FLORA**, and the 10-gun **VICTOR**, spied them and gave chase. The **FOX** was recaptured by the British, and the **HANCOCK** was forced to surrender, but the **BOSTON** made it safely into Maine. British Commodore George Collier, commander of the **RAINBOW**, brought Manley with his ship and crew into Halifax,

Nova Scotia. *"We are fortunate to get this man into our possession,"* announced Collier, and the HANCOCK, which he renamed H.M.S IRIS, he said *"is the finest frigate in the world."* In August of 1781, the IRIS, former HANCOCK, captured the Connecticut frigate TRUMBULL. The BOSTON had to anchor at Boston for a few months, for Congress, believing that McNeill should have come to Manley's aid, *"suspended him, pending a court-martial."* He was later *"dismissed from the navy."* Unfortunately, around this same time, another of America's first warships, the CABOT, was captured off Nova Scotia by the H.M.S. MILFORD, and was towed into Halifax as another British prize. An added catastrophe for the American Navy was that the British managed to occupy Newport, Rhode Island without opposition on December 7, 1776 and controlled Narragansett Bay with 14 men-of-war, blockading the remainder of America's fleet, including the new frigates WARREN and PROVIDENCE stuck in the Providence River.

Abe Whipple, taking command of the new 28-gun PROVIDENCE, and turning his old command of the COLUMBUS over to Hoystead Hacker, tried many times to slip through the British blockade, but each time had to retreat back into the river. Hacker attempted to break free in the COLUMBUS, but was cornered by a British flotilla off Point Judith, Rhode Island, and was forced to run her into shore and abandon her. The WARREN, under command of John Hopkins, made it through the blockade in March of 1778, but after taking a few enemy merchant ships and returning to port, Hopkins was accused of illegally taking prize money and was relieved of his command. Whipple, in the PROVIDENCE, snuck out of Narragansett Bay and into the open sea on April 30, *"running the gauntlet by 11 British warships."* He managed to capture three rich merchantmen carrying what was considered the most valuable cargoes taken during the war. The PROVIDENCE was finally captured by the British the following year during the fall of Charlestown, as was the frigate BOSTON. The WARREN, with Dudley Saltonstall in command, and the sloop PROVIDENCE, were purposely destroyed by their own crews in August of 1779 to avoid capture by the British at Penobscot, Maine, during the disastrous *"Battle Of Castine."* Included in this rout and destruction of 42 American vessels by six British frigates under command of Sir George Collier, were four vessels of the Massachusetts Navy, one Connecticut ship, one New Hampshire ship, 12 American privateers, and 21 transport barges that carried 1,000 militiamen and marines to battle the British held Fort George at Castine, Maine. All 42 vessels were either purposely destroyed by their crews to avoid capture, or were destroyed by the British squadron. Some 500 sailors, militiamen, and marines were captured or killed, but the British lost only 15 men. The survivors were forced to walk back to Boston through the Maine wilderness. Paul Revere, in charge of artillary, was demoted in rank for not following orders, and Commodore Dudley Saltonstall, who ran instead of attacking the British ships, was court-martialed and kicked out of the American Navy — some congressmen suggested that he should be shot. At the time, Secretary of State and War, Timothy Pickering of Salem understated, *"our Naval affairs are shocking and our Commanders are shamefully bad."*

Although Congress had decided to build more warships in late 1776 and in 77, of the total 35 vessels purchased and built during these years, 21 of them were destroyed or captured by the enemy by January 1781. Eleven were still fighting, but for the wrong side, and only three still waved the stars and stripes. Many of them were built in New England, but after the **WARREN** and **PROVIDENCE**, Rhode Island was omitted from the congressional list of ship builders, not only because of the British blockade at Newport, but because of allegations that Rhode Islanders were misappropriating federal funds. John Brown of **GASPEE** fame, for example, had fitted out the **WARREN** with weak rigging and rotting ropes. He was also responsible for setting her masts, which toppled over before she had even set sail. Cost overruns, delays, and steep wages demanded by ship-builders and riggers, came close to *"requiring Congress to mortgage the entire continent,"* as Samuel Chase of Maryland had predicted. To avoid national bankruptcy, many new ships ordered to be built by Congress were never completed. One that did make it down the ways in Portsmouth, New Hampshire in 1777 was the 18-gun corvette (small frigate) **RANGER**, commanded by John Paul Jones. Another, launched the following year at Salisbury, Massachusetts, was the 32-gun frigate **ALLIANCE**. Of the 53 naval vessels bought, borrowed, or built by the Provincial Congress during the Revolutionary War, the only one still afloat and still in the American Navy at the end of the war, was the **ALLIANCE**. Her glory as a fighting ship came while under the command of John Barry, but under her first commander Piere Landais, a Frenchman who claimed to be an honorary citizen of Massachusettts, the **ALLIANCE** was a failure, and even twice attempted to sink John Paul Jones' ships from right under him. During a shakedown cruise the **ALLIANCE** smashed into the **RANGER**, causing a seaman aboard the **RANGER** to fall from the rigging, knocking Jones' hat off his head, and the crewman hit the deck, dead. Both ships were damaged, and the angry little Scot, who New Hampshire claims as her adopted son, cursed Commander Landais, and accused the Frenchman of colliding with the **RANGER** on purpose.

John Paul, who went to sea as a cabin-boy at age twelve and was captain of the brig **JOHN O'GAUNT** at age 19, inherited a Virginia plantation in 1773 through the death of his brother William. The plantation had been owned by the Jones family— thus he adopted that name as his own. As commander of the **PROVIDENCE** and **ALFRED**, he had captured 22 enemy ships and Congress appointed him commander of the **RANGER** on June 14, 1777. That same day Congress resolved that America's new flag would be *"thirteen stripes, alternate red and white, and that the Union be thirteen stars in a blue field, representing a new constellation."* Jones remarked, *"the flag and I are twins, born the same hour, from the same womb of destiny."* When the **RANGER** departed Portsmouth, New Hampshire for France, five local ladies of the *"Helen Seavey Quilting Party"* presented him with the new American flag, which they had pieced together from old dresses. When the **RANGER** sailed into Quiberon Bay, on February 14, 1778, the French fleet gave the new flag a nine-gun salute — this was the first recognition of an Independent America from a foreign nation.

Within two months, working out of the port of Brest, the **RANGER** captured four British merchant vessels carrying valuable cargoes, and sank two more in battle. On April 22nd, at midnight, Jones attacked the coast of England, landing 30 marines in two boats at Whitehaven. Jones led one party and assaulted a seaside fort, spiking 36 cannons, then burned five ships that were anchored in the harbor. The marines in the second boat destroyed a gun battery, but were forced to retreat when the Whitehaven militia showed up. Next, Jones sailed for Scotland's shores, planning on the capture of the Earl of Selkirk, but when the marines raided his estate, the Earl wasn't at home. The **RANGER** crew stole the family silver instead. Lady Selkirk was upset to say the least, but she thought Marine Lieutenant Sam Wall was *"well mannered,"* but she said that the short 5'6" commander John Paul *"had a vile blackguard look."* The 24-gun sloop-of-war **DRAKE** had been out for weeks searching for the **RANGER**, and she encountered her sailing back to France from the Selkirk estate. Within one hour of close combat, the British commander and his first lieutenant were killed and the **DRAKE** surrendered. She was towed into Brest by the **RANGER**. A two month cruise had brought the crew one million dollars in prize money. Even the 14 year old **RANGER** cabin-boy received $1,400 and also *"a ton of sugar, 80 lbs of food and clothes, and 35 gallons of rum."* Jones also brought in 200 British prisoners.

The French now offered Jones command of a 40-gun ship, which he accepted, turning over the **RANGER** to Thomas Simpson. Simpson sailed her back to America and she was captured by the British at the fall of Charlestown, South Carolina in May of 1780 along with the **PROVIDENCE** and the **BOSTON**. The British renamed the **RANGER** the **HALIFAX**. Jones in his **LE BON HOMME RICHARD** provided America with the greatest sea victory of the Revolution on September 22, 1779. He was Commodore of a squadron which included the **ALLIANCE**, the 36-gun **PALLAS**, and the 32-gun **VENGEANCE**, commanded by Frenchmen, with crews of *"every conceivable nationality,"* including Swiss, Swedes, Irishmen and Spaniards. Within a few weeks at sea, off the coast of England, they captured ten merchant vessels and destroyed 16 more at anchor in the port of Hull. The people of Sunderland, England were so panic-stricken that they packed up their belongings and moved inland, and then, off Flamborough Head, Jones met the entire British Baltic Fleet. Leading this fleet of merchantmen, were the 54-gun British men-of-war **SERAPIS** and the 22-gun **SCARBOROUGH**. Jones, whose ship was almost half the size of the double-decked **SERAPIS**, headed straight for her. The **PALLAS** took on the **SCARBOROUGH**, and the British merchant vessels scattered. The **ALLIANCE** and **VENGEANCE** were sailing too far behind to initially join in the battle. It was 7:00 p.m. when Jones fired his first broadside, but when he did, six of the **RICHARD**'s cannons burst, killing and wounding many of his own men. The **SERAPIS** answered with a series of broadsides. Jones sailed the **RICHARD** in close to bump the **SERAPIS**, and with grappling irons, his crew lashed the two ships together. Carrying muskets and grenades, Jones' men swung from the **RICHARD**'s rigging onto the enemy ship and dropped grenades to the deck, killing many cannoneers. Sharpshooters shot at the British deck officers, killing most of them, while the cannons on both sides, with muzzles touching each other, were rendered useless. A last volley by the **SERAPIS**, however, blew through the **RICHARD**'s hull and she started to sink. Jones sent over a boarding party of marines carrying pikes and cutlasses, and as Commander Richard Pearson of the **SERAPIS** later reported, *"the Americans gained full possession of the forepart of my ship."* Said Jones, *"No action before was ever in all respects so bloody, so severe and so lasting."*

During the heat of the battle the **ALLIANCE** arrived on the scene and sent a broadside into the **SERAPIS**, *"but to my astonishment,"* said Jones, *"Commander Landais discharged a broadside full into the stern of the RICHARD as well, and then another broadside into my forecastle. Then he retreated."* This was not a mistake by Peter Landais. He was jealous of Jones. He later confided to a friend that he hoped to sink the **RICHARD**, then board the **SERAPIS** and become the hero of the day. At his subsequent court-martial, he testified that it was so dark that he couldn't tell the ships apart from each other, and thereby he escaped punishment. Commander Pearson shouted to Jones, *"Have you struck your colors.... Do you ask quarter?"* — then Jones made his famous reply: *"Hell no! I have not yet begun to fight."* Both ships were on fire and the battle raged on until 10:30 p.m. *"Then,"* Pearson later testified, *"I seized the ensign halyards and struck the **SERAPIS** flag myself."* Jones quickly had all his men board the **SERAPIS**, for the **RICHARD**, with her American flag still flying, was about to go under. *"The last vistage mortal eyes ever saw of the **BON HOMME RICHARD**,"* said Jones, *"was the defiant waving of her unconquered and unstricken flag as she went down."* She had taken a British man-of-war almost twice her size— this was a first, not only for the Americans, but for the British. Although neither commander ever officially listed their casualties, Commander Pearson commented that *"the **RICHARD** had 306 men killed or wounded, and our loss on the **SERAPIS** was also very great."* The **PALLAS** also defeated the **SCARBOROUGH** in a two hour battle, and when the commander and crew returned to France, they were given a heroes welcome. The French government, however, kept the **SERAPIS** as a prize of war, and although Jones wanted to command her, he had to take Landais' place as commander of the **ALLIANCE**. When Commander Pearson was allowed to return home to England, the King knighted him for his bravery in the fight against the **RICHARD**. On hearing this Jones said, *"If I ever fall in with him again, I'll make him a Lord."* Jones, who is considered the greatest naval hero of the Revolutionary War, died of natural causes in Paris in 1792. His body, *"miraculously preserved, except where the casket had pressed his nose,"* was dug up in 1905 and he was reburied in American soil at the Naval Academy, Annapolis, Maryland. That same year, Encyclopedia Britannica still listed John Paul Jones as *"a pirate."*

Although American Naval ships captured some 200 enemy vessels during the war, 25% of them by Jones, only 13 were British warships— the money and effort expended on an American Navy weren't worth the results. George Washington's rowboats and sailboats were more successful, as were New England's privateers, capturing and destroying thousands of enemy vessels at little expense to the nation. Congress, in fact, collected an estimated $20 million from British cargoes captured by privateersmen. Except for Barry and Jones, America's heroes were privateersmen— although some of them were naval commanders who left military service for privateering. Captain John Manley, after the **HANCOCK** was captured, languished in a British prison until 1782 when he was released in a prisoner trade. When he returned home to Boston, he opted to become a privateer commander and not return to the

Continental Navy. In the privateer **JASON**, he captured two merchant vessels with rich cargoes valued at twice what it cost to build the lost **HANCOCK**. Jonathan Haraden of Salem, who first commanded the Massachusetts Navy brig **TYRANNICIDE**, resigned his naval commission in 1780, stating that he didn't like *"the stiffness of the navy."* He then commanded the 14-gun privateer **GENERAL PICKERING**, and as historian William Clark wrote, *"he probably did more in this capacity to win the war than any one of a dozen generals in the Continental Army, Washington, of course, excepted."*

Salem privateersmen alone captured and safely brought into port 445 British prizes, and 62 of them were brought in by Haraden, carrying over 1,000 cannons and 3,000 British prisoners-of-war. *"His enemies believed that he was watched over by evil spirits,"* said Clark, *"so great was his success and so amazing his victories."* His second in command aboard the **PICKERING**, John Carnes, said that *"Haraden fought with a determination that seemed superhuman."* On one of his voyages in the **PICKERING** he took three British vessels at one time, *"managing to manouver so as to meet them seperately."* On a subsequent cruise, he captured a 16-gun British warship, a 14-gun sloop and a 14-gun brig, within two weeks. Heading toward the West Indies in the **PICKERING** he met one of King George's well armed mail packets. It was 20-cannons and an 80-man crew against Haraden's 14-guns and 40 men. Haraden attacked her and the two ships pounded each other for four hours, *"only once hauling off for repairs."* Haraden then brought the **PICKERING** alongside the packet. He had one charge of powder left, which was crammed into one cannon. *"I will give you five minutes to haul down your colors and surrender,"* he shouted to the British commander, *"and if you don't, I'll sink you, so help me God."* Haraden held a watch in his hand and counted aloud. The commander surrendered before Haraden had counted a minute. *"He was master of the bluff,"* said Carnes, *"cool, quiet, happy and carefree."* Once, using painted canvas and screens, he covered his gunports and disguised the **PICKERING** as an unarmed merchant vessel. Two British warsloops came in for the kill, and Haraden slipped off the canvas, giving them both a series of broadsides until they surrendered.

Off Bilbao, Spain, a favorite hangout for American privateersmen, the **PICKERING** eased up one evening aside the 22-gun British schooner **GOLDEN EAGLE**. *"Strike your colors or I'll sink you,"* shouted Haraden to the surprised British commander. It was so dark that the commander couldn't see that the **PICKERING** was half the size of his vessel. To Haraden's delight and surprise, the British commander immediately surrendered. Haraden placed ten of his men as prize crew aboard the **GOLDEN EAGLE**, but bringing her into Bilbao, the 40-gun British ship **ARCHILLES** attacked both vessels. The **GOLDEN EAGLE** was recaptured, but the **PICKERING** dueled the big ship for three hours. *"The **PICKERING** looked like a longboat beside the great ship **ARCHILLES**,"* reported Cowen, *"yet Haraden was all the time calm and steady where the shot flew around him in the thousands, as amidst a shower of snowflakes."* The towering British ship had trouble giving an effective broadside because the **PICKERING** sat so low in the water. Haraden was a genius at maneuvering a ship in battle, and all the time he moved in and out of the shallows where the **ARCHILLES** commander dare not tread. Haraden, stuffing his cannons with crowbars and shot, peppered the big ship, causing such heavy damage that the **ARCHILLES** heeled and ran. Haraden chased her for three hours but couldn't catch up to finish her off. He did however recapture the **GOLDEN EAGLE**. Haraden was undoubtedly the greatest privateersman who ever lived.

Another who came close to Haraden's feats of valor was Silas Talbot, who sailed out of Providence, Rhode Island at age 14 as a cabin-boy. Still in his teens when the Revolution erupted, he joined Washington's Army and was twice wounded and severely burned when he tried to fire-bomb the British 64-gun warship **ARGUS** in the Hudson River. Recuperating from his wounds at home in Providence, he assisted General John Sullivan in his futile attempt to retake Newport from the British in August of 1778. Fitting out an old scow merchant vessel with two cannons and 60 volunteers, he drifted down the river and smashed into the British schooner **PIGOT**. Talbot led a boarding party that forced 50 marines to retreat below deck, and the **PIGOT**'s commander Dunlap, *"in his underpants"* begged for mercy and surrendered. Talbot sailed the **PIGOT** to Stonington, Connecticut, where he received a hero's welcome. George Washington then put him in charge of the 12-gun sloop **ARGO** to patrol the waters off Connecticut and Rhode Island. In quick succession, Talbot, with his initial volunteers, took the 12-gun **LIVELY**, 14-gun **KING GEORGE**, 10-gun **ELLIOT**, 14-gun **DRAGON**, and 14-gun **HANNAH**. On his second cruise in Long Island Sound, he took three more enemy ships, but then met up with the 30-gun British ship **RAISONNABLE**, which gave **ARGO** such a broadside that she was crippled and had to limp back to port. Talbot then commanded the **GENERAL WASHINGTON** which battled two British ships successfully, but was captured by the **H.M.S CULLODEN**, and Talbot was finally confined to a British prisonship.

With the help of the French fleet, Washington won Lord Cornwallis' surrender at Yorktown in October, 1781, but the war on the sea didn't end until Congress proclaimed victory on April 11, 1783 some 17 months later. Coincidentally, the news of the signing of the peace treaty in England was brought to America by the ship **ASTREA** and her skipper was John Derby, the same man who brought England the news eight years before that the war had started. A few days later, his brother Elias Derby's famous privateer **GRAND TURK** arrived in Salem, and with her was a large British ship **POMPEY** that she had taken off England. The **POMPEY** commander and crew hadn't put up a fight, for they heard the news that the war was over, but the **GRAND TURK** men had no such news, so they brought her back to Derby as a prize. Elias Derby kept her as a prize of war and renamed her **AMERICA**. The **POMPEY** is considered the last British ship taken during the Revolutionary War, but actually the last taken was the British ship **MARTINICO** by the Salem privateer **PORUS**. She arrived in port on May 28, 1783, 47 days after the war was over. Her skipper allowed the cargo to scatter throughout New England, for the **MARTINICO** carried 200 African slaves.

When Congress authorized the first American Navy battle cruisers to be built after the war in 1794, the man chosen to command the greatest American Navy vessel ever known was the former Providence cabin-boy and privateersman Silas Talbot. The ship was constructed and launched at Boston in 1797. The following year, Congress officially instituted the United States Navy, and Silas Talbot took the **U. S. S. CONSTITUTION** to sea. Her first prize was in 1799, the French frigate **L'INSURGENTE**, and 13 years later *"Old Ironsides"*, under command of Issac Hull, became the heroine of America's second successful war with Britain, The War of 1812. Her many victories overshadowed the great disappointments and defeats experienced by the American Navy in the previous war, and but for the *"pirates,"* as the British called privateersmen, there might have been few victories at sea during the Revolution. Washington himself admitted at Valley Forge that *"without a constant naval superiority upon these coasts, the stuggle will be over."* It was men of the Naughty Navy like O'Brien, Tupper, Manley, Mugford, Glover, Whipple, Barney, Barry, Biddle, Hill, Haraden, Jones, and Talbot, who turned America's greatest stuggle on the high seas into victory and gave us what we so dearly cherish today — our freedom.

(Bibliography available by writing the publishing company.)